R. Lambert Playfair

The Bibliography of the Barbary States

Part I - Tripoli and the Cyrenaica

R. Lambert Playfair

The Bibliography of the Barbary States
Part I - Tripoli and the Cyrenaica

ISBN/EAN: 9783337143404

Printed in Europe, USA, Canada, Australia, Japan

Cover: Foto ©ninafisch / pixelio.de

More available books at **www.hansebooks.com**

THE

BIBLIOGRAPHY

OF

THE BARBARY STATES.

PART I.

TRIPOLI AND THE CYRENAICA.

(*WITH A MAP*).

BY

SIR R. LAMBERT PLAYFAIR, K.C.M.G.,

H.M. CONSUL-GENERAL FOR ALGERIA AND TUNIS;

AUTHOR OF 'TRAVELS IN THE FOOTSTEPS OF BRUCE'; 'THE SCOURGE OF CHRISTENDOM';
'HANDBOOK (MURRAY'S) TO ALGERIA AND TUNIS';
'HANDBOOK (MURRAY'S) TO THE MEDITERRANEAN,' ETC.

THE BIBLIOGRAPHY

OF

THE BARBARY STATES.

PART I.—TRIPOLI AND THE CYRENAICA.

By Lieut.-Col. Sir R. Lambert Playfair, k.c.m.g., etc.

—————

All that now remains of the three Eastern Barbary States is a Bibliography! Tripoli is a vilayet of the Turkish Empire, and eager eyes are turned towards this part of the Sick Man's inheritance. Tunis is a French Protectorate, and in the natural course of things will one day lose the last shred of its independence. The "famous and warlike city of Algiers" is the capital of a French colony, a prolongation of France. Morocco alone retains its independence and much of its mystery; in spite of its unrivalled position, its ports on either ocean, its perennial streams fed by snow-clad mountains, and its brave and hardy population, it still remains as impenetrable to modern civilisation as ever. But it also has its "question," though the writer hopes to complete its Bibliography before it too "joins the majority."

The complete Bibliography of the Barbary States will contain the following parts:—

I. *Tripoli and the Cyrenaica*, the subject of the following pages.

II. *Tunisia*, by Messrs. Graham and Ashbee, forming originally an appendix to their excellent book of travels,* but which they purpose publishing in a separate form completed to a later date.

III. *Algeria*, already published by the writer in part 2, vol. 2, of the

---

* 'Travels in Tunisia,' with a glossary, a map, a bibliography and fifty illustrations. By Alexander Graham, f.r.i.b.a., and H. S. Ashbee, f.s.a., f.r.g.s.; London: 8vo.; Dulau & Co., 37, Soho Square, 1887.

R. G. S. Supplementary Papers for 1888, pp. 132-430, but requiring a supplement.

IV. *Morocco*, in progress.

The Province of Tripoli is less known to the general public than the three others, and a map has been thought likely to prove serviceable to the student of its literature. It extends along the coast from the island of Djerba to Tobrook, a little beyond the Bay of Bomba, rather more than 800 miles, including all the territory between Tunis and Egypt. Southward it comprises the territory of Fezzan, the town of Ghadames, and the oasis of Ghat. Along the coast, and to about seventy miles inland, there are fertile tracts, but beyond this limit the country is for the most part a barren desert, interspersed at intervals with a few oases.

Nevertheless, it contains many spots of more than ordinary interest, celebrated by the poets and historians of Greece and Rome. The shores of the Syrtis were the terror of navigators, both in ancient and more modern times. Tripoli is the ancient Oea, which, with its neighbouring cities of Leptis and Sabrata, constituted a federal union styled Libya Tripolitana. Beyond this is Cyrenaica, or the Pentapolis, so named from its five Greek cities, Barca, Teuchira, Hesperis, Cyrene and its harbour Appolonia. Under the Ptolemies, Hesperis became Berenice, the modern Bengazi; Teuchira was called Arsinoë, the modern Taucra; and the port of Barca was raised into a city by the name of Ptolemais, the modern Tolemeta./ The capital of all this district was Cyrene, the most important Hellenic city in Africa, founded B.C. 631. It gave its name to a well-known philosophic sect, and was the birthplace of many distinguished people, while in commercial importance it almost rivalled Carthage;/its cities were adorned with magnificent edifices, and its fountains and forests became the scene of many interesting mythological events. Here were the "dull forgetful waters" of Lethe and the garden of the Hesperides. The army of Cato nearly found a grave in the sands between it and Leptis Magna, and Oea, the capital of the Syrtica Regio, was the birthplace of some of the most prominent characters in Roman history.

Beyond the Cyrenaica and extending to the borders of Egypt was Marmarica, a sandy region stretching inland as far as the oasis of Jupiter Ammon.

After the destruction of Carthage, Tripoli became a Roman province, the coast line subsequently passed into the hands of the Vandals, from whom it was rescued by Belisarius. Then came the most extraordinary movement which the world has ever seen, the sudden rise and extension of Mohammedanism, following the death of its founder, which obliterated every trace of Christianity and civilisation from North Africa.

Since then, with rare and short intervals, Tripoli has remained in the hands of the Mohammedans, the government of the caliphs being succeeded by various local dynasties, and finally it passed into those of the Sultan in 1835.

This is not the place for a detailed historical or geographical account of the country. The student will find all that can be said on these subjects, though perhaps an *embarras de choix*, in the works herein catalogued.

No attempt at a systematic rendering of oriental names is possible ; authors must be held responsible for the orthography of the words used by them.

A BIBLIOGRAPHY

OF

TRIPOLI AND THE CYRENAICA.

1. B.C. 484. **Herodotus.**—See Nos. 96, 266.

2. B.C. 350. **Scylax of Caryanda.**—See No. 96.

3. A.D. 20. **Strabo.**—See Nos. 96, 202.

4. 41. **Mela, Pomponius.**—See No. 24.

5. 77. **Pliny** the Elder.—See Nos. 96, 248.

6. 160. **Ptolemy.**—See No. 96.

7. 160. **Antoninus Augustus.**—See Nos. 94, 96, 216.

8. 238. **Solinus Polyhistor.**—See No. 96.

9. 413. **Paulus Arosius.**—See No. 96.

10. 527. **Procopius of Cæsarea.**—See No. 55.

11. 630. **Isodorus of Hispalis.**—See No. 96.

12. 970. **Ibn Haukal.**—See Nos. 124, 200.

13. 1050. **El-Bekri.**—See No. 267.

13A. 1100. **El-Edrisi.**—See No. 185.

13D. 1300. **En-Noweiri.**—See Nos. 196, 210, 215.

13C. 1330. **Abu 'l Feda, Ismäel.**—See Nos. 118, 119, 121, 190, 194, 199.

14. 1355. **Ibn Batuta.**—See Nos. 168, 238, 239.

15. 1356. **Treaty of Peace and Commerce** between Ahmed Ibn-Mekki, Lord of Tripoli, &c., and the envoy of Venice. Mas-Latrie, Traités, D. pp. 222. See No. 326.

16. 1358. **Protest** and declaration of reprisals of Marco Venier, Venitian ship-owner, against the acts of the Lord of Tripoli. Mas-Latrie, Traités, D. pp. 228.

17. 1362. **Letter of Credence** from Laurentius Celsi, Doge of Venice, to Pierre Sante, Ducal Notary, charged with a Mission to Tripoli. Mas-Latrie, Traités, D. pp. 230.

18. 1375. **Ibn Khaldun.**—See No. 215.

19. 1510. **Sanudo, Marino,** Diary of.—Preserved in the Archives of Venice. Mas-Latrie, Traités, D. pp. 256.

Amongst other interesting matter this contains a letter dated 29th July, 1510, in which Don Pedro Navarro, commanding a Spanish force, reports having taken Tripoli.

20. 1510. Ferdinand of Arragon, writing to Henry VIII., informs him that Piedro Navarro stormed Tripoli on the 25th July, with great slaughter. 10,000 of the enemy were slain and the rest taken. Calend. State Papers, For. and Dom. Henry VIII., vol. 1, 1509-1511, No. 1209.

21. 1510. Privilege awarded by Ferdinand to the Merchants of Barcelona to trade at Tripoli and Bougie. Mas-Latrie, Traités, D. pp. 336.

22. 1512. New Privilege granted by Ferdinand to the inhabitants of Catalonia to trade at Tunis, Algiers, Tripoli and Bougie. Mas-Latrie, Traités, D pp. 341.

23. 1524. Tripoli granted by Charles V. to the Knights of Rhodes upon certain conditions. Calend. State Papers, Ven. Ser. 1520-1526. 797-799.
From the original letter-book in St. Mark's Library.

24. 1543. Pomponius Mela.—De Situ Orbis. Libri Tres, Basiliae, folio. Many other editions, amongst others,—Opera et Studio, J. Reinoldii, Eton, 4to. 1814. Collection des Auteurs Latins avec la traduction en Français publié par M. Nisard ; Macrobe, Varron, Pomponius Mela. Paris : 1845, 8vo, pp. 709.
Mela flourished about the middle of the first century. He examines the three divisions of the globe known to the ancients, and describes Mauritania ; Numidia, with its capital, Cirta ; Africa, with its cities, Hippone, Rusicada, Utica, Carthage, etc., Leptis, Lake Triton, the Island of the Lotophagi, Oea, the modern Tripoli, and the Cyrenaica with the oasis of Jupiter Ammon.

25. 1551. Tripoli taken by the Turks. Calend. State Papers, Foreign Ser., vol. 1547-1553, ed. vi., pp. 163, 165, 170, 172.
" Letters from the Grand Master announce the surrender at discretion of Tripoli ; that M. d'Aramon had saved 200 men of 'note, that the rest of the soldiers, about 500, were put in chains, and others fit for the oar were impressed."

26. 1552. Salazar y Murdones, P.—Hystoria de la guerra y pressa de Africa ; con la destruycion de la villa de Monatzer y isola del Gozo, y perdida de Tripol de Berberia.
Napoles. fol.

26A. 1553. Villegagnon, Nicolas Durand de.—Le discours de la guerre de Malte, contenant la perte de Tripolis et autre forteresses faussement imposée aux Français. Escrit en Latin a Charles V. par le Seigneur Nicolas de Villegagnon, puis traduit en nostre vulgaire par M. N. Edoard. Lyon : 8vo, pp. 123.

27. 1556. Leo Africanus. — De Totius Africæ Descriptione, libri ix. Antwerpiae, 1556 ; Zurich, 1559 : 8vo.
The author was an Arab of Granada, named El-Hassan bin Mohammed El-Ouezaz El-Gharnathi, who visited a great part of Africa. He was taken by Corsairs, and baptised by Leo X. His original work was in Arabic, but it has been translated into Latin and into nearly all the modern languages of Europe. The English version bears the title : A Particular Treatise of all the Maine lands and Isles described by John Leo, with map. London : 1600, 4to. A French translation, by Jean Temporal, was published at Lyon, 1556, folio ; and an Italian version is given in Ramusio, vol. 1.

The French edition was re-published at Paris at the cost of Government in 1830: 4 vol. 8vo, pp. xlviii., 640; 581; viii., 758; xxiii., 576. The first book treats of Africa in general; the second and third are devoted to Morocco and Fez; the fifth, sixth and seventh refer to various parts of Algeria, Tunis, Tripoli and the Cyrenaica.

Though Leo was a native of Granada, he went to Africa at a very early age and studied at Fez and Morocco; visited Timbuctou and many parts of the Barbary States before his conversion to Christianity. An interesting biographical sketch of this remarkable man is given by Berbrugger, Rev. Afr. vol. ii. 1858, p. 353.

28. 1560. **Views of Tripoli.**—Two very curious views of Tripoli about this date exist. One is in the British Museum (Press Mark 642, 10). The other is in the Public Record Office (see No. 1 of the Tripoli Archives). Both show the Quadrifrontal Arch entire and separate, and in the latter the town is being besieged by the army of Philip of Spain. Both are probably published at Venice, and the former is ascribed to D. Zenoi.

29. 1560. **Cirni, Ant. Fr.**   Successi dell' Armata Catholica destinata all' impresa di Tripoli de Barbaria.   Venetia: 8vo.   Reprinted at Florence in 1567. 8vo.

30. 1561. **Naval engagement** between the Galleys of Philip of Spain and the Morres of Tripoli, in which the former were vanquished. Calend. State Papers—1561-1562, 300.

31. 1561. **Carrelières, Th. de.**   Histoire de l'entreprise de Tripoli et prise de Gerbes par les Chrestiens en 1559.   Lyon: 12mo.—See also Calend. State Papers, London.   Foreign 1559-60, 859.—1066.—l.c. 1560-61, 450, 564.

32. 1566. **Ulloa, Alphonso de.**   La historia dell' impresa de Tripoli di Barberia, della presa del Pegnon di Velez della Gomera in Africa et del successo della potentissima Armata Turchesca venuta sopra l'isola di Malta, l'anno 1565. Venetia: 4to, pp. 87.   With a preface by G. B. Tebaldi.   A second edition. Venetia: 4to, 1569.

33. 1568. **Bertelli, F.**   Civitatum aliquot insigniarum, &c.   Ven.: 4to. A collection of prints, one of which is of Tripoli.

34. 1568. **Nicolas de Nicolai,** Segnieur d'Artefeuilte.   Ses premiers quatre livres des navigations et peregrinations orientales.   Lyon: folio, pp. 181, with numerous illustrations.

The author was Valet de chambre and Geographer in Ordinary to King Charles IX.   There are many editions.   Chap. xviii. treats of the "Fondation de la Cite de Tripoly."

35. 1573. **Marmol-Caravajal, L.**—Descripcion General de Affrica. Con todos los succsos de guerras que a avido entre los infieles y el pueblo christiano. Granada: 2 vols. folio.

Marmol was a native of Granada, served in the expedition of Charles V. against Algiers, was taken prisoner, and travelled during seven years and eight months over a great part of North Africa. A French translation was published by d'Ablancourt at Paris in 1667, 3 vols. 4to, pp. 532, 578, 304. Tripoli is described under the heading "Regno de Tvnez. Libro sexto," vol. 2.

36. 1581. **A Treaty** between France and Turkey, dated 6th July, renewed the capitulation with Sultan Amurat, therein styled Sovereign of Algiers, Tunis and Tripoli.   See Tab. des Etab. Franç. en Alg. 1841, p. 416.   See No. 195.

37. 1583. **Sanders, Thomas.**—See Hakluyt; also published separately at London in 1587 : 4to.

38. 1588. **Sanuto, M. Livio.**—Geografia distinta in xiii. libri, &c., con xii. tauole di essa Africa in dissegno di rame.
Venezia, folio, pp. 146, with a copious index and 12 maps. Only one vol. was ever published. At pp. 64-66 is a description of Tripoli and the Cyrenaica.

39. 1588. **Marcellinus, Ammianus.**—Lives of the Emperors from Constantine to Valens and Gratian. V. Sylburgius Historiæ Romanæ Scriptores Latini minores. vol. ii. Also, Collection des Auteurs Latins avec la traduction en Français. M. Nisard, Paris : 1849.

40. 1597. **A Treaty** between Henry IV. of France, and Sultan Mahomet III. of Turkey, dated 25th Feb., confirmed the privileges granted to ambassadors, consuls and merchants in the Levant and Barbary, specifying Algiers, Tunis and Tripoli, and conceded the Coral Fishery to France. See Tab. des Étab. Franç. en Algérie, 1841, p. 416.

41. 1599. **Hakluyt, Rev. Richard.**—The Principal Navigations, Voyages, Traffiques, and Discoveries of the English Nation made by sea or overland, to the remote and furthest distant quarters of the earth, at any time within the compasse of these 1600 yeres, &c. London : folio, 2 vols. pp. 620, 312—204. B.L.
Vol. ii. part i. contains The English Voyages made by and within the Streight of Gibraltar.
The following have reference to Tripoli :—

42. Page 177. A Letter of the English Ambassadors (W. Hareborne) to M. Edward Barton, enclosing the next-named "Commandement."

43. Page 177. The Commandement of the Grand Signior, obtained by Her Majesties Ambassador, M. Will. Hareborne, for the quiet passing of her subjects to and fro his dominions, sent in 1584 to the Viceroys of Algier, Tunis and Tripolis in Barbary.

44. Page 178. A Letter of the Hon. M. Will. Hareborne, Her Majesties Ambassador with the Grand Signior, to M. Tipton, appointing him Consul of the English in Algier, Tunis and Tripolis of Barbarie, dated 30th March, 1585.— Tipton had already held this position at Algiers in an unofficial manner, for some time.

45. Page 184. The voyage made to Tripolis in Barbarie, in the yeere 1583, with a ship called the *Jesus*, wherein the adventures and distresses of some Englishmen are truely reported, and other necessary circumstances observed. Written by **Thomas Sanders.** This voyage was under the auspices of the Turkish Company. The vessel was plundered, the master, Andrew Dier, was hanged, and the crew were doomed to slavery, and only released owing to the intercession of Queen Elizabeth at the Sublime Porte.

46. Page 191. Correspondence regarding the restitution of the shippe called the *Jesus* and the English captives detained in Tripolie in Barbarie and for certain other prisoners in Argier. 1584.
A new edition, with additions, was published in 1809 and following year. This work has recently been reprinted by Messrs. E. & G. Goldsmid, of Edinburgh.

48. 1603. **Knolles, Richard,** Fellow of Lincoln's College, Oxford.—The General History of the Turkes, from the first beginning of that nation to the rising of the Othoman Familie, with all the notable expeditions of the Christian Princes against them, &c. London : folio, pp. 1152.

The history is followed by "a brief discourse of the greatness of the Turkish Empire."

49. 1610. **Tonsis, Battistino de.**—Historia della guerra di Tripoli di Barbaria.

50. 1614. **Purchas, Samuel.**—His Pilgrimage, or relation of the world and the religions observed in all ages and places, &c. London : 9 books, in 1 vol. folio, pp. 1047.

Chapter viii. of the 6th book treats of 'that part of Barbarie now called the Kingdom of Tunis and Tripoli.' With map. Several other editions.

51. 1620. **Mala, Petro.**—Relazione della presca fatta ai Turchi dalle galere di Francia in Barberia. 8vo.

52. 1625. **Purchas, Samuel,** "Parson of St. Martins neare Ludgate."—His Pilgrims in 5 bookes (4 vols.). London : folio, pp. 1973.

At vol. ii. p. 874. The Description of Alger, written by Nicholas Nicholay, . . . and also of Malta and Tripolie.

53. 1649. **Dan, Le Rev. P. Fr. Pierre,** Supérieur de l'ordre de la S. Trinité au Chasteau de Fontaine-bleau.—Histoire de Barbarie et de ses corsaires, des royaumes, et des villes d'Alger, de Tunis, de Salé et de Tripoli. Paris : folio, pp. 489.

From p. 250 to 255 is more especially devoted to Tripoli. There were but few slaves there in the author's time.

54. 1650. **Birago Avogadro, Dr. Gio. Batt.**—Historia Africana, della divisione dell' Imperio degli Arabi. E dell' origine e dei progressi della Monarchia de' Mahometani distesa per l'Africa e per le Spague. Venitia : 4to, pp. 445.

P. 300, Tripoli confederata di Algieri.

P. 324, Tripoli posseduta da Goti.

—— A French translation by M[ichel] d[e] P[ure]. Paris, 1666, 18mo, pp. 262.

55. 1653. **Procopius of Cæsarea.**—Several editions of the original exist, and one English translation by **Sir Henry Holcroft.**—History of the Warres of the Emperour Justinian, 8 books. London : folio, 1653.

This translation is exceedingly rare. No copy exists in the British Museum or the Advocates' Library in Edinburgh ; there is one at the Bodleian, and another at Aberdeen.

56. 1654. **Chaulmer.**—Le tableau de l'Afrique où sont représentés les royaumes, républiques, principautés, iles, presqu'iles, forts, &c., de cette seconde partie du monde. Paris : 12mo, pp. 359.

Chap. II. Section V. treats of Tripoli, the Cyrenaica and the Marmarica.

57. 1654. **Tabula Peutingeriana,** ex edit. G. Harini, Amst. See Appendix to Shaw, No. 96. Also 'La Table de Peutinger d'après l'original conservé à Vienne, par Ernest Desjardins.' Paris : 1869.

58. 1655. **Sanson, Nicolas,** d'Abbeville.—Partie de la Coste de Barbarie en Afrique, où sont les Royaumes de Tunis et de Tripoli et pays circonvoisins, tirés de Sanuto. Paris : 4to. No pagination. See No. 19.

59. 1660. A Chart or View of Tripoli.—Showing an attack made by boats on a large vessel in the harbour. A drawing, coloured, in the King's Collection, Brit. Mus. (cxvii. 61.) This is followed by another pen-and-ink view of the same town (cxvii. 62).

60. 1662. Treaty of Peace between Great Britain and Tripoli, signed by Sir John Lawson, 18th October, 1662. Hertslet's Treaties, vol. i. p. 125.

61. 1667. De Voornaemste Steden der Werelts.—The Principall Citties of the World ; known as G. van Schagen's collection. Amsterdam : oblong 4to.

Two of the prints, one with the legend in French, represent Tripoli. The latter is the same view as that given in Mortier, No. 86.

62. 1668-70. Dapper, O.—Naukerige Beschryvinge der Afrikaenschen Gewesten von Egypten, Barbaryen, Libyen, Biledulgered, Negroslant, Guinea, Ethiopia, Abyssinie. Amsterdam : folio. French translation published 1686, folio. German translation, 1670. See also Nos. 63, 75.

Part iii. treats of the Barbary States, including Tripoli and Barca ; part iv. of the Belad et Djerid, and part v. of Libya. It contains a curious view of Tripoli.

63. 1670. Ogilby, John.—Africa : being an accurate description of the regions of Egypt, Barbary, Libya, and the Billedulgerid, etc. Folio, maps and plates.

A mere translation of Dapper. The author is a very miscellaneous writer, but an unconscientious plagiarist.

64. 1675. Treaty of Peace and Commerce between Great Britain and Tripoli, signed by Sir John Narborough, 5th March, 1675-76. (Renewed by Article xxv. of the Treaty of 1716.) Hertslet's Treaties, vol. i. p. 128.

65. 1676. Hollar, W.—Links oben Tripoli in Barbary. A separate print. See Parthey, No. 1203. Very rare.

66. 1675. Seller, John, Hydrographer to the King.—Atlas Maritimus, or the Sea Atlas, being a book of Maritime Charts describing the sea-coasts, capes, headlands, etc., in most of the known parts of the world. London : folio. One of them is a bird's-eye view of Tripoli, coloured, engraved by Hollar.

67. 1676. Relatione del Nuovo incendio seguito alli 24 di febrero 1676 tra le navi inglese et quelle de Tripoli de Barbaria. Milano : 4to.

68. 1676. Narrative of the burning of four men-of-war at Tripoli. London : folio.

69. 1685. A Treaty was signed between France and Tripoli after the bombardment of the latter town by the Duc d'Estrées. The Tripolitans restored 600 Christian slaves, two French vessels, and paid a large indemnity. Tab. des Étab. Franç. en Alg. 1841, p. 420.

70. 1685. Tripoli le 16 Maggio, 1685. Distinto Raggeruglio gionto per lettera particolare ad un Mercante nel porto d' Ancona. Roma, Modena, Parma : Sm. 4to, p. 3.

An account of various phenomena which appeared at Tripoli, and the sufferings of some Christian slaves at the hands of the Mohammedans, contained in a collection of tracts in the Brit. Mus., Press mark : $\frac{9135.\ cc.\ 1.}{(1-55.)}$

71. 1687. Knolles, Richard. The Turkish History from the original of that Nation to the growth of the Ottoman Empire, with the lives and conquests of their Princes and Emperors. With a continuation to this present year, 1687, by Sir Paul Rycant, eighteen years consul at Smyrna. London: folio, 3 vol., pp. 990, 338-606.

At vol. ii. p. 136 is "State of the affairs of England in reference to . . . . Algiers and other parts of Barbary."

72.   1688.   Petit de la Croix.—Relation Universelle de l'Afrique Ancienne et Moderne. Lyon: 4 vol. 8vo.; and 1713.

73.   1694.   Additional Articles between Great Britain and Tripoli, signed by Thomas Baker, late Consul-General, 11th October, 1694. Hertslet's Treaties, vol. i. p. 136, and Calend. Treas. Papers, 1557-1696, p. 392.

74.   1694.   Schauplatz barbarischer Slaverei, oder, von Algier, Tripoli, Tunis, und Salee. Hamburg: 8vo, pp. 124.

75.   1695.   A collection of prints in the British Museum, Press mark S. 148 (38), contains some most interesting views of places in Africa. Published probably in Amsterdam. The legends are in Dutch and English. No. 5 represents Tripoli. There are also views of Algiers, Djidjeli and Tunis. The volume has no letterpress or title. ? Dapper. No. 63.

76.   1700.   Godefroy, Père, Comelin et Philemon de la Motte, missionnaires de la très Sainte Trinité et Rédemption des Captifs. Etat des Royaumes de Barbarie, Tripoly, Tunis et Alger, contenant l'histoire naturelle et politique de ces Pais; la maniere dont les Turcs y traitent les esclaves, comme on les rachete; et divers avantures curieuses. Avec la Tradition de l'Eglise pour le rachat ou le soulagement des Captifs. Rouen: 12mo, pp. 263, 270.

The first letter, pp. 1 to 90, is " Etat Chrétien et politique du Royaume de Tripoli," and contains an interesting account of the state of Christian Slavery there. Other editions published at La Haye, 1704, and at Rouen, 1731.

77.   1700.   Glorioso triumfo conseguido por quatro galeras de la religion de S. Juan en los mares de Berberia, apressando un vaxel de Tripoli llamado *Sultana,* al 9 de Octobre de 1700. Barcelona.

78.   1702.   P. Schenkii, Hecatompolis sive totius orbis Terrarum oppida nobiliora centum. Amsterdam: obl. 4to.

A collection of coloured engravings, of which one (89) represents Tripoli.

79.   1705.   Harris, John, A.M. Navigantium atque Itinerantium Bibliotheca, or a complete collection of voyages and travels, consisting of above four hundred of the most authentic writers; beginning with Hakluit, Purchas, &c., in English; Ramusio in Italian; Thevenot, &c., in French; De Bry and Grynæi Novus Orbis in Latin; the Dutch East India Company in Dutch; and continued with others of note, &c., &c.   London: 2 vol. folio, pp. 862, 928 and [App.] 56.

Ch. xii. contains . . . a short account of Malta and Tripoli; taken from Nicholas Nicolay.

80.   1708.   Allerneuster Zustand der Afrikanischen Königreiche Tripoli, Tunis, und Algier, von einem gelerten Jesuiten. Aus dem Französischen. Hamburg: 8vo, pp. 124.

81.   1712.   Lucas, Paul. Voyage du Sieur Paul Lucas, fait par Ordre du Roy, dans la Grèce, l'Asie Mineure, la Macédoine et l'Afrique. Description de l'Anatolie, la Caramanie, la Macédoine, Jérusalem, l'Egypte, le Fioume, et un Mémoire pour servir à l'histoire de Tunis, depuis 1684.   Paris: 12mo, 2 vol. illustrated. pp. 410-417.

Ch. x. vol. ii. describes his visit to Mesurata and Tripoli. Chap. xi. a voyage in the mountains of Derna, Cyrene, Bengazi, &c.

82. 1715. **Van der Aa, Pierre.**—La Galerie Agreable du Monde ou l'on voit en un grand nombre de cartes et de Belles Tailles-Douces, les principaux Empires, &c. Le tout mis en ordre et exécuté à Leide: sm. folio.

Plates Nos. 13a and 14 are copies of those previously noticed. No. 75. No. 15 is "Manière de Supplicier les esclaves à Tripoli." The vol. also contains some interesting views of Algiers and Tunis.

83. 1716. **Treaty between Great Britain and Tripoli,** signed by Vice-Admiral John Baker, 19th July, 1716. Hertslet's Treaties, vol. i. p. 137.

84. 1718. **Rowe, Nicholas.** Lucan's Pharsalia, translated into English verse. London : folio, pp. xxv. 446–55.

In Book ix. is an account of Cato's gathering the remnants of the Battle of Pharsalia, and transporting them to Cyrene ; a description of the Syrtis follows, and a digression concerning the Temple of Jupiter Ammon.

85. 1720. **Treaty** between the Bey of Tripoli and France, 4th July and 19th Aug., in favour of French commerce. Tab. des Étab. Fr. en Alg. 1841, p. 422.

86. 1720 (?) **Les Forces de l'Europe,** Asie, Afrique et Amerique, ou description des principales Villes avec leurs fortifications. Dessignées par les Meilleurs Ingenieurs, &c. Amsterdam : 4to.

No. 158 represents Tripoli, a mere sketch outline evidently copied from Van Schagen's collection. This one is published by Pierre Mortier.

87. 1724. **Vera** ... relazione della battaglia seguite in mare tra un vascello corsaro Tripolino e le galere della sagra Religione di Malta con la presa di detto vascello. In Lucca ed in Bologna : 4to.

88. 1725. **Laugier de Tassy, N.**—Histoire du Royaume d'Alger. Amsterdam : 12mo, maps.

The author was Commissaire de la Marine for the King of Spain in Holland. His work was pirated in English by Morgan in 1728 and 1750, and it has been translated into several other languages.

It was also pirated in French, 'État Général et particulier du Royaume et de la ville d'Alger, et de son gouvernement, &c.' La Haye: 1750, 12mo. A new edition of the original work was published in 1732 under the title: 'État d'esclavage des Chrétiens au Royaume d'Alger avec celui de son gouvernement, &c.' Amsterdam : 8vo, pp. 300. The author copies freely from Marmol. A Spanish edition was published at Barcelona in 1733, pp. 340, with maps and view of Algiers.

89. 1729. **Treaty** between France and Tripoli, dated 9th June.* Tab. des Étab. Fr. en Alg., 1841, p. 422.

90. 1731. **Godefroy, le P.**—Etat des Royaumes de Barbarie, Tripoly, Tunis et Alger ; contenant l'histoire politique et naturelle de ces païs—La manière dont les Turcs y traitent les esclaves, comme on les rachète et diverses aventures curieuses—Avec la tradition de l' Église pour le rachat des captifs. Rouen : 12mo.

91. 1731. **Condamine, de la.**—Voyage en Barbarie et eu Orient. MS. Bibliothèque Nationale, Paris.

* Confirmed on the 30th June, 1793.

92. 1732. Cellarius, Christophorus.—Notitiae orbis antiqui, sive geographiae plenoris Tomus alter Asiam et Africam antiquam exponens.   Vol. ii. Lipsiae : 4to, pp. 970.
Lib. iv. cap. ii. p. 838, De Marmarica et Pentapoli Cyrenaica. Cap. iii. De Regione Syrtica.   Cap. iv. De Africa Propria, sev. Carthaginiensi.   He mentions that no part of the coast of Africa was called *Tripolis* till the close of the 1st century.

93. 1733. Hebenstreit, J. E., Professor of Medicine at the University of Leipzig.—De Antiquitatibus romanis per Africam repertis. Leipzig : 4to.

94. 1735. Antonini Augusti Itinerario.—See Appendix to Shaw, No. 96.

95. 1735. D'Arvieux, Le Chevalier, Consul d'Alep, d'Alger et de Tripoli.—Mémoires de .... mis en ordre par le R. P. Jean-Baptiste Labat, de l'ordre des Frères Prêcheurs. Paris : 6 vol., 12mo.
At vol. 5, p. 413 is "Mémoire presenté au Roi pour reprimer l'insolence des Corsaires de Tripoli d'Afrique et pour les forcer à une paix avantageuse aux sujets de S. M."

96. 1738. Shaw, Thomas, D.D., F.R.S., Fellow of Queen's College, Oxford.—Travels and Observations relating to several parts of Barbary and the Levant. Oxford : folio, pp. xv., 442, 60 ; second edition, 4to.
Dr. Shaw was chaplain to the Consulate at Algiers. This is one of the most valuable works ever written on North Africa.   See ' Quarterly Review,' vol. xcix. p. 331.
He does not allude to Tripoli, but in an Appendix he gives :—Sylloge excerptorum ex veteribus Geographis Historicis, &c., or a collection of such extracts from the old Geographers, Historians, &c., as chiefly relate to that part of Africa or Barbary known by the name of the Kingdom of Algiers and Tunis, as follows :—Herodoti Halicarnass Histor., Libro iv., Lug. Bat. 1715. Scylacis Caryandensis Periplo, Oxon. 1698. Strabonis Rerum Geographicae, Libris ii. et xvii., Amst. 1619.   Cl. Ptolemæi Geographiæ, Libro iv. et viii., Amst. 1619. Pomponio Mela, De Situ Orbis, Iscæ Dumnon., 1711. C. Plinii Secundi Hist. Naturalis, Libro v., Par. 1685. J. Solini Polyhistore, Traj. ad Rhen. 1685. Antonini Aug. Itinerario, Lug. Bat. 1738. Æthici Cosmographia, Lug. Bat. 1696. J. Honorii Oratoris excerptis, ibid. Sexti Rufi Breviario Hist. Romanæ, Hanov. 1611. Pauli Orosii Adversus Paganos Historia, Col. 1582. Martiani Minei Felicis Capellæ de Nuptiis Philosophiæ, Lib. vi., Bas. 1577. Isidori Hispalensis Originum, Lib. xiv., ibid. Collatione Carthaginensi, Notitia Episcoporum Africæ sub Hunerico, Concilio Carthaginensi sub Cypriano, &c.; sive Notitia omnium Episcopatuum Ecclesiæ Africanæ ; quæ præfigitur S. Optuli de Schism. Donatistarum Libris septem, opera et studio M. Lud. Ell. Du Pin, Antuer. 1702. Notitia utraque Dignitatum cum Orientis tum Occidentis, ultra Arcadii Honoriique tempora, Lugd. 1608. Ravenate anonymo, Amst. 1696. Tabula Peutingeriana, ex edit. G. Hornii, Amst. 1654. [This table, which is indispensable for students of the Ancient Geography of North Africa, has been reproduced in autograph from the original MS. in the Imperial Library at Vienna by B. Chambrier, "Commis auxiliaire au Secrétariat du Conseil de Gouvernement du Gouvernement Général de l'Algérie."]
Shaw's work was translated into French, and published at La Haye, 1743, 2 vol. 4to, carte et figures; and into German, and published at Leipzig, 1765, 4to.

97. 1740. **Bodenehr, G.**—A collection of prints without any published title, Augsberg: fol. Press mark in Brit. Mus., S. 148 (38).
Two of these represent Tripoli.

98. 1740-1751. **An Universal History,** from the earliest times to the present, compiled from original authors and illustrated with maps, cuts, notes, chronological, and other tables. London: folio, 8 vol.
Vol. vii. chap. 7. The history of the Libyans and Greeks, inhabiting the tract between the borders of Egypt and the River Triton, comprehending Marmarica, Cyrenaica, and the Regio Syrtica.

99. 1742. **Tollot, Le‾Sieur.**—Nouveau voyage fait au Levant, ès années 1731-1732, contenant les descriptions d'Alger, Tunis, Tripoly de Barbarie, &c. Paris: 8vo, pp. 354. See also Piesse Rev. Afr. vol. xi. p. 417.
The author merely touched at Tripoli on his way from Algiers and Tunis to Egypt.

100. 1746. **Hardion, M.**—Histoire de la Ville de Cyrène. Hist. de l'Acad. Roy. des Inscr. et Belles Lettres, t. 3, pp. 391–413. Read 17th Dec., 1715.
Commences an account of the ancient history of Cyrene taken from classic authors. M. Hardion died before it was completed. See No. 113.

101. 1750. **A compleat history** of the Piratical States of Barbary, viz. Algiers, Tunis, Tripoly, and Morocco. Containing the origin, revolutions, and present state of those kingdoms, their forces, revenues, and policies and commerce. With a plan of Algiers and a map of Barbary, by a gentleman (Morgan) who resided there many years in a public character. 8vo.
This was translated into French by Boyer de Prebandier in 1757. The work is of little value; it is a mere translation of Laugier de Tassy, who again copied from Marmol. Morgan was an indefatigable plagiarist.

102. 1750. **Historical Memoir of Barbary,** and its Maritime Power, as connected with the Plunder of the Seas; including a sketch of Algiers, Tripoli and Tunis, an account of the various attacks made upon them by the several States of Europe, considerations on their present means of defence, and the original treaties entered into with them by Charles II.
Another edition published at London in 1815.

103. 1751. **Treaty between Great Britain and Tripoli,** signed by the Hon. Augustus Keppel, Commander-in-Chief in the Mediterranean, and Consul-General Robert White, 19th Sept., 1751.—Hertslet's Treaties, vol. i. pp. 143.

104. 1751. **Nauze, M. de la.**—Histoire du Calendrier Egyptien. Hist. de l'Acad. Roy. des Inscr. et Bell. Lett., t. 16, pp. 170.
At p. 181 is an account of an inscription said to have been taken to France from Tripoli, which had been originally placed in the Amphitheatre of Berenice by the Magistrates and Jews.

105. 1754. **Fréret, Nicolas.**—Observations sur l'époque d'une ancienne Inscription grecque apportée de Tripoli d'Afrique en Province et placée dans le Cabinet de M. le Bret. Hist. de l'Acad. Roy. des Inscr. et Bell. Lett. t. 21, pp. 35–225.
This is a decree of the Jews of Berenice ordering an eulogium on M. Titius every new moon.

106. 1754. **Istoria degli Stati di Algeri,** Tunisi, Tripoli e Marocco. Trasportata fedelemente dalla lingua Inglese nell' Italiano. In Londra: 12mo, pp. 376.

107. 1756. **Fréret, M.** Observations sur le rapport des Mesures Grecques et des Mesures Romaines. Mem. de Litt. tirés des Reg. de l'Acad. Roy. des Inscr. and Bell. Let., t. 24, pp. 548–568.

At. p. 554 is a comparison of the measures in the Cyrenaica.

108. 1757. **Histoire des États Barbaresques** qui exercent la Piraterie. Contenant l'origine, les révolutions et l'état présent des Royaumes d'Alger, de Tunis, de Tripoli et de Maroc. Par un auteur (Morgan) qui y a résidé plusieurs années avec caractère public. Traduit de l'Anglois par Boyer de Prebandier. Paris : 2 vol. 18mo, pp. 388 and 287. See No. 101.

109. 1762. **Treaty between Great Britain and Tripoli**, signed by Archibald Cleveland, Esq., H.B.M. Ambassador to the Emperor of Fez and Morocco, on the 22nd July 1762. Hertslet's Treaties, vol. i. p. 151. Cal. State Papers Dom. Ser. 1760–1765, No. 623.

110. 1764. **Anderson, Adam.**—An Historical and Chronological Deduction of the Origin of Commerce. London : 2 vol. folio.

This gives an account of the establishment of Consuls, of whom John Tipton of Algiers, Tunis and Tripoli was one of the first ever appointed.

111. 1766. **Harrison, Commodore Thos.** His Mission to Tripoli. See Cat. Home Office Papers. 1766–69. Nos. 123, 176.

With the original documents (15½ pp.) is a well-executed plan and survey of the harbour of Tripoli.

112. 1771. **Monro, Dr. Alexander.**—Of a pure native crystalised natron or fossil alkaline salt, found in the Country of Tripoli in Barbary. Phil. Trans. Abr. xiii. p. 216.

113. 1774. **Belley, L'Abbé.** Observations sur l'histoire et sur les Monumens de la ville de Cyrène. Mem. de Litt. tirés des Reg. de l'Académie Royale des Inscr. et Bell. lett. t. 37, pp. 363–390.

This is a continuation of M. Hardion's Account, see No. 100.

114. 1775. **Schloezer, August Ludwig von.**—Summarische Gesch. v. Nord-Africa, namentlich, von Marocko, Algier, Tunis und Tripoli. Göttingen, 8vo, pp. 93.

Very little of this work is devoted to Tripoli.

115. 1776. **Borg, Antonio.**—" Piano del Porto di Tripoli e fortificazioni," drawn on a scale of 150 paces to an inch, with a " prospettiva della città di Tripoli." Add. MSS. Brit. Mus. 13, 950, 76.

116. 1781. **Hebenstreit, Joannes Ernestus.**—Vier Berichte von seiner auf Befehl Friedrich Augusts I. im Jahre 1732 in Begleitung einiger anderer Gelehrten and Künstler auf den Afrikanischen Küsten nach Algier, Tunis und Tripolis angestellten Reise.—See J. Bernouillis Sammlung Kurzer-Reisebeschreibungen, &c., Bd. 9–12; also Eyriès, Nouv. Ann. des Voyages, t. xlvi. 1830. pp. 1–90.

117. 1785. **Voyage** dans les États Barbaresques de Maroc, Alger, Tunis et Tripoly, ou lettres d'un des captifs qui viennent d'être rachetés par MM. les Chanoines réguliers de la Sainte Trinité, suivies d'une notice sur leur rachat et du catalogue de leurs noms. Paris : 12mo.

This gives a list of 313 captives redeemed.

118. 1789. **Ismail ibn Ali** (Abu 'l Feda).—Abulfedae Annales Muslemici Arabice et Latine opera et studiis J. J. Reiskii. Nunc primum edidit J. G. C. Adler. Hafniae : 1789–94. 4to.

119. 1790. **Ismail ibn Ali** (Abu 'l Feda).—Ismaclis abulfedae annalium Moslemicorum excerpta, quae ad Historiam Africanam et Siculam spectant sub imperio Arabum. Folio. Arab. and Latin.

120. 1790. **Bruce, James.**—Travels to discover the source of the Nile in 1768–1763. Edinburgh: maps and plates, 5 vols. 4to.

This contains a notice of his explorations in Algeria, Tunis, Tripoli and the Cyrenaica before starting for Sicily, Baalbec, Palmyra and subsequently Egypt. A French translation published in Paris, translated by J. Castera in 1790–91.

121. 1791. **Ismail ibn Ali** (Abu 'l Feda).—Abulfedae Africa. Curavit I. G. Eichhorn. Arab. Gottingae: 8vo.

122. 1794. **A Short Account of Algiers,** and of its several Wars ... with a concise account of the origin of the rupture between Algiers and the United States. Philadelphia: 8vo, pp. 50.

123. 1800. **Rennel, Major James,** Surv. Gen. Bengal.—The Geographical System of Herodotus examined and explained by a comparison with those of other ancient authors and with Modern Geography. In the course of the work are introduced ... The oasis and Temple of Jupiter Ammon, the ancient circumnavigation of Africa, &c. London: 4to, pp. 766, with 11 maps.

Sect. xxii. Of the Tribes who inhabited the coast and country of Libya between Egypt and Carthage. Sect. xxiii. Concerning the two Syrtes; the Lake Tritonis, &c. Map ix. The coast and country of Libya.

124. 1800. **Ibn-Haukal.**—The Oriental Geography of Ibn Haukal, an Arabian Traveller of the 10th Century, translated by Sir W. Ouseley. London: 4to.

125. 1801. **Treaty** between France and Tripoli, dated 19th June, containing the "most favoured nation" clause. Tab. des Étab. Fr. en Alg. 1841, p. 423.

126. 1802. **Horneman, Frederick.**—Journal of travels from Cairo to Mourzouk the Capital of the Kingdom of Fezzan in Africa, in the year 1797–8. London: 4to, pp. 195, with 2 maps.

The author was employed by the Society for Exploring the Interior of Africa. He went direct from Cairo to Mourzouk, and thence to Tripoli, whence he returned to Mourzouk.

Also a French translation, Paris, 1803, 2 vol. 8vo, with valuable notes by Langles principally from Arab authors.

127. 1802–3. **Cuny, C.**—Tableau historique des decouverts et établissements Européens dans le nord et l'ouest de l'Afrique, jusqu'au commencement du xix Siècle, augmenté du Voyage d'Horniman dans le Fezzan, et de tous les renseignements qui sont parvenus depuis à la Société d'Afrique sur les empores du Bornou, du Kashna, &c. Traduit par Cuny. Paris: An. xii., 8vo.

128. 1805. **W. E.** (William Eaton)—Interesting details of operations of the American fleet in the Mediterranean. Letter from W. E., an officer, to his friend in the county of Hampshire (Mass.). Springfield: 8vo, pp. 32.

129. 1806. **History of the War** between the United States and Tripoli, and other Barbary Powers, to which is prefixed a Geographical, Religious and Political History of the Barbary States in general. Printed at the Salem Gazette office, Salem, U.S.A.: 12mo, pp. 144.

In an appendix is given a letter from General William Eaton to the Secretary of the Navy, dated 9th Aug., 1805.

130. 1808. **Murray, Alexander.**—James Bruce; account of his life and writings. Edinburgh: 4to, maps and plates.

131. 1812. **Treaty between Great Britain and Tripoli,** signed by Captain Mathew Smith, H.M.S. Comus. 10th May, 1812. Hertslet's Treaties, vol. i. p. 152.

132. 1813. **Blaquière, Edward.**—Letters from the Mediterranean; containing a civil and political account of Sicily, Tripoli, Tunis and Malta; with Bibliographical Sketches, &c. London: 8vo, 2 vol. pp. 652, 460.

The first 105 pp. of vol. 2 are on Tripoli.

A German translation: Briefe aus dem Mittelländischen Meere, forms vols. xxv. and xxvi. of 'Neue Bibliothek der wichtigsten Reisebeschreibungen,' &c., von F. J. Bertuch, &c. Weimar: 1815–35, 8vo, 65 vol., maps and engravings.

133. 1813. **Eaton, General William,** Life of. — Brookfield, U.S.A.: 8vo, pp. 448.

At p. 301 is an extract from his journal relating to his march from Alexandria through the desert to Derna.

134. 1813. **Biography of Commodore Decatur.**—The Analectic Maga. Philadelphia: vol. i. p. 502.

135. 1814. **Ali Bey el Abbassi,** Pseudonym of D. Badia y Leblich, a Spanish traveller.—Voyages en Afrique et en Asie pendant les Années 1803–1807. Paris, 3 vol. 8vo, with atlas, long folio, lxxxiii. plates, of which the first, from i. to xii. bis, relate to Morocco. xiii. to xv. relate to Tripoli.

An English version was published at London, 1816, 2 vol. 4to, and a second French edition at Paris, 1884, 3 vol. 12mo.

The author travelled as a Turk; he landed at Tangier, where he saw the Sultan, passed through Meknos to Fez, where he resided a winter, returned to the coast at Laraiche, where he embarked for Tripoli, and the further East.

Vol. i. chap. xxii. contains an account of Tripoli, with a plan of the great Mosque and copies of several Roman inscriptions.

136. 1816. **Treaty between Great Britain and Tripoli,** signed by Lord Exmouth, 29th April, 1816. Hertslet's Treaties, vol. i. p. 153.

Placing the inhabitants of the Ionian Islands on the same footing as natives of Great Britain.

137. 1816. **Declaration,** signed by the Bey of Tripoli at the instance of Lord Exmouth, providing for the abolition of Christian Slavery, l. c. p. 155.

It is curious that nothing exists on this subject in the Tripoli Archives.

138. 1816. **Janson, W.**—A View of the Present Condition of the States of Barbary; or an account of the Climate, Soil, Produce, Population, Manufactures, Naval and Military strength of Morocco, Fez, Algiers, Tripoli, and Tunis. Also a Description of their Mode of Warfare, interspersed with anecdotes of their Cruel Treatment of Christian captives, illustrated by a new and correct hydrographical map, drawn by J. J. Asheton.

This gives an account of the American War on Tripoli, and of Eaton's expedition from Egypt to Derna.

139. 1816. **Historical Memoirs of Barbary,** as connected with the Plunder of the Seas; including a sketch of Algiers, Tripoli and Tunis, an account of the various attacks made upon them by several States of Europe; considerations of their present means of defence; and the original treaties entered into with them by Charles II. London: 12mo, pp. 112.

The portion devoted to Tripoli and Barca is from pp. 53 to 58. It is without value.

140. 1816. Hunt, Gilbert T.—The late War between the United States and Great Britain from June 1812 to February 1815, written in the ancient historical style : containing also a sketch of the late Algerine War, and the Treaty concluded with the Dey of Algiers. New York : 8vo, pp. 334.

The whole work is a poor travesty of Biblical language, very partial to the U.S., and generally untrustworthy, being a mere compilation.

See also two articles in the Analectic Review, Philadelphia, vol. vii. pp. 105–113 and 113–131. The former gives a sketch of the Barbary States ; the latter narrates Decatur's expedition against Algiers, Tunis and Tripoli, which proved successful where European fleets had failed.

141. 1816–17. Marcelli, Steph. Ant.—Africa Christiana. Brixiae : 3 vol. 4to, pp. 394, 376, 341, with maps of Mauritania, Numidia and Tripolita.

This is the great standard work on the African Church.

142. 1817. Dümgé, Dr. C. G.—Ansichten von Tripoly, Tunis und Algier, aus dem Reiseberichten Französischen Missionairs. Stuttgart : 8vo. pp. 120.

143. 1817. Tully, Richard.—Narrative of a ten years' residence at Tripoli in Africa, from the original correspondence in the possession of the family of the late Richard Tully, Esq., the British Consul. Written by his Sister. London : 4to, pp. 370, with map and 6 coloured plates.

Reviewed in the Monthly Review, 1818, vol. lxxxvii. pp. 113–121, and the Christ. Observer, vol. xvi. pp. 453–467.

144. 1817. Leyden, John, and Hugh Murray.—Historical account of Discoveries and Travels in Africa . . . with illustrations of its Geography and Natural History as well as the moral and social conditions of its inhabitants. 2nd edition. Edinburgh : 2 vol. 8vo, pp. 512–535.

Vol. i. p. 296, contains an abstract of Mr. Lucas' journey from Tripoli to Fezzan ; p. 417, Horneman's journey to Jupiter Ammon, Fezzan and Tripoli. Vol. ii. p. 209, Voyage of the *Jesus* to Tripoli ; p. 230, Shaw's travels in Barbary ; p. 252, Tully's Tripoli ; at p. 521 there is a bibliography of important works relating to Africa.

The original edition was published in 1799, and a French translation by Cuvillier appeared in Paris, 4 vol. 8vo, with atlas, in 1821.

145. 1818. Declaration of the Bey of Tripoli, forbidding his vessels from cruising near any British Port. Signed by Consul-Gen. H. Warrington, 8th March, 1818. Hertslet's Treaties, vol. iii. p. 27.

146. 1819. Della Cella, Paolo. Viaggio da Tripoli di Barberia alle Frontieri occidentali dell' Egitto, fatto nel 1817 dal Dottore Paolo Della Cella, e scritto in littera al Sig. D. Viviani. Genoa : 8vo.

An English translation was published at London, 1822 : 'Narrative of an Expedition from Tripoli in Barbary to the Western Frontier of Egypt in 1817 by the Bey of Tripoli, in letters to Dr. Viviani, of Genoa, by Paolo Della Cella, M.D., Physician Attendant of the Bey ; with an appendix containing instructions for navigating the Great Syrtis. Translated from the Italian by **Anthony Aufrere, Esq.**' London : 8vo, pp. 238. Reviewed in Quart. Rev. vol. xxvi., 1822, pp. 209–229, and in Edin. Rev. vol. xlviii., 1828, pp. 220–235.

Also a French edition : 'Voyage en Afrique au royaume de Barca et dans la Cyrénaïque,' traduit par **A. Pezaut.** Paris, 1840.

The author gives an animated description of what he saw, but his work is superficial.

147. 1821. Lyon, Capt. G. F., R.N.—A narrative of Travels in Northern
Africa in the years 1818, 1819 and 1820. Accompanied by geographical notices
of Soudan, and the course of the Niger. London : 4to, pp. 383, map, and 17
coloured plates.

> The author accompanied Mr. Ritchie, who was employed by the British
> Government, on a mission to Central Africa, where he died. He started from
> Tripoli, and travelled as far south as 24° N. lat.
>
> A French translation by L. Ed. Gauthier was published in Paris, 1882,
> 2 vol. 12mo.
>
> See also Tripoli Archives, No. 17.

148. 1821. Walckenaer, C. A., Membre de l'Institut.—Recherches géographiques
sur l'intérieur de l'Afrique Septentrionale, comprenant l'histoire des Voyages
entrepris ou exécutés jusqu'à ce jour pour pénétrer dans l'Intérieur du Soudan, &c.
Paris : 8vo, pp. 525, with a map.

> Part iii. p. 249 et seq. contains an account of the various routes inland
> from Tripoli. See also Journ. des Savants, 1822, p. 104.

149. 1821. Niles, John M.—The life of Oliver Hazard Parry, with an appendix
comprising a biographical memoir of . . . . Commodores Bainbridge and Decatur.
Hartford, U.S. : 12mo, pp. 384.

> Bainbridge commanded the *Philadelphia*, which ran ashore at Tripoli, when
> he and his crew were made prisoners. Both were distinguished in the Barbary
> War.

150. 1821. Hutton, Catherine.—The tour of Africa, containing a concise
account of all the countries in that quarter of the globe hitherto visited by
Europeans. London : 3 vol. 8vo.

> Written as if by an imaginary traveller.   Vol. iii. p. 468 et seq. refers to
> Tripoli.

151. 1824. Jomard.—Découvertes récentes en Afrique nouvelles tirées du
Quarterly Review, Dec. 1823. Bull. Soc. Géogr. Paris, t. 2, p. 11.

152. 1824. Viviani, D.—Florae Libycae Specimen. Folio. Genoa.

153. 1825. Hamaker, H. A.—Lettres de M. H. Arent. Hamaker à M. Raoul
Rochette sur une inscription en caractères phéniciens et grecs récemment découverte à Cyrène. Leyde : 4to, lithographed, 1 plate.

**154. 1826. Denham, Major, Captain Hugh Clapperton, and the late
Dr. Oudney.**—Narrative of Travels and Discoveries in Northern and Central
Africa, in the years 1822, 1823 and 1824. Extending across the Great Desert to
10° N. Lat., and from Kouka in Bornou to Sackatoo, the capital of the Felatah
Empire. London : 2 vol. 8vo, 3rd edition, 1828, pp. 471, 465, with maps, plates,
and illustrations.

> An American edition was published in Boston, 1 vol. 8vo, pp. lxiv. + 255
> + 104 + 112.
>
> The authors started from Tripoli, and the two first returned to the same
> place.—See also Tripoli Archives.

155. 1826. Letronne, J. Ant.—Rapport de la Commission nommée par
l'Académie pour examiner les résultats du voyage en Cyrénaïque et en Marmarique, par M. Pacho. Journ. des Sav. pp. 166-170.

> Project of publication of Pacho's work, l. c. p. 505.

156. 1826. **Malte-Bruin, M.** —Rapport des Commissaires nommés par la Commission Centrale de la Soc. de Géogr. pour examiner les résultats du voyage de M. Pachô dans la Cyrénaïque. Bull. Soc. Géogr. Paris, t. 5, pp. 558-576. The Society voted him the prize of 3000f.

157. 1826. **Gråberg da Hemsö, Count J. C.,** Danish Consul at Tripoli.— Letter from Tripoli. He gives news of Major Gordon Laing. Bull. Soc. Géogr., Paris, t. 5, p. 680.

158. 1829. **Pachô, Raymond.** —Relation d'un voyage dans la Marmarique, la Cyrénaïque, et les Oasis de d'Audjelah et de Maradeh, pendant les années 1824 et 1825 ; accompagnée de cartes géographiques et topographiques et de planches représentant les monuments de ces contrées. Paris : 4to, 1827-1829, pp. 404, atlas, fol., 3 maps, and 100 plates.

159. —— Rapport des Commissaires nommés par la Commission Centrale pour examiner les resultats de voyage de M. Pachô dans la Cyrénaïque.

160. —— Notice sur la Cyrénaïque lue à la Soc. de Géogr.

161. —— See also Edin. Rev., vol. xlviii. 1828, pp. 220.

162. 1827. **Gråberg da Hemsö, Comte J. C.,** Swedish Consul.—Commercio di Tripoli. Antologia; Giornale delle Scienze. Florence : 1827, 1828 and 1830. Nos. 81, 88, 111.

Reviewed in the London Magazine, 3rd ser., vol. ii., October 1828, pp. 361-366, under the title " An Account of the Present State of Tripoli." The author states that Tripoli was in a more advanced condition than any of the other Barbary States on account of the hereditary forms of its government.

163. 1827. **L'Investigateur Africain.**—A journal published at Tripoli during a short period, to which M. J. L. Rousseau, French Consul, was a contributor. It was edited by Gråberg de Hemsö.

164. 1828. **Lyman, Theodore.**—The Diplomacy of the United States, being an account of the foreign relations of the country from the first treaty with France to the present time. Boston: 2nd edition, with additions, 2 vol. pp. xii. 470, xii. 517.

Vol. ii. chap. xiii. relates to negotiations with the Barbary Powers, including operations at Tripoli and Eaton's expedition.

165. 1828. **Thrige, J. P.,** Scholae Roeskildensis.—Res Cyrenensium a primordiis inde civitatis usque ad aetatem, qua in provinciae formam a Romanis est redacta; novis curis illustravit J. P. T. a schedis defuncti auctoris, edidit **S. N. J. Bloch.** Hafniae : 8vo, pp. 371.

The texts concerning the history of Cyrene taken from Herodotus, Pausanius, Scylax, &c., are brought together. The first edition was published in 1819.

166. 1828. **Beechey, Capt. F. W., and H. W. Beechey.**—Proceedings of the expedition to explore the Northern Coast of Africa from Tripoli Eastward in 1821-22. Comprehending an account of the Greater Syrtis and Cyrenaica, and of the ancient cities composing the Pentapolis. London : 4to, pp. xxiv. 572, xlviii., with 9 maps and 13 plates.

Reviewed in Edin. Rev., vol. xlviii., 1828, p. 220.—See also Tripoli Archives, No. 19. A most exhaustive work.

167. 1828. **Laing, Major Gordon.**—An account of his travels from Tripoli to Timbuctoo and murder near the latter place is given in the Quarterly Review, vol. xxxviii. p. 100.—See also a French translation of this article in the Biblio-thèque Universelle, Genève, 1828, t. xxxix. p. 47.—Also Tripoli Archives, Nos. 23, 26, 27, 30, 31, 32.

168. 1829. **Lee, Samuel, D.D.**—The travels of **Ibn Batuta,** translated from the abridged manuscript copies in the Public Library of Cambridge. Printed for the Oriental Translation Committee. London : 4to, pp. xviii. and 242.

Chap. i. treats of Tangiers, Tilimsān, Milyāna, Algiers, Bijāya, Kosantina, Būna, Tūnis, Sūsa, Safākus, Kābis, Tripoli, &c.

Ibn Batuta left his native city, Tangier, about 1324, and spent two years in making his journey.

169. 1830. **Head, Major F. B.**—The life of Bruce, the African traveller. London : 12mo, pp. 535, with portrait and maps.

At p. 47 is an account of Bruce's travels in Tripoli and shipwreck at Benghazi.

170. 1830. **Jameson, Prof., James Wilson,** and **Hugh Murray.**—Nar-rative of discovery and adventure in Africa, from the earliest ages to the present time. Edinburgh : 12mo, pp. 492.

This gives a *résumé* of the explorations of Horneman, Laing, Ritchie and Lyon, with a general account of Africa. It forms vol. ii. of the Edinburgh Cabinet Library.

171. 1830. **Russell, Rt. Rev. M.,** Bishop of the Scotch Episcopal Church, Glasgow and Galloway. History and Present Condition of the Barbary States, forming vol. xvii. of the Edin. Par. Lib. Edinburgh : 8vo, pp. 448.

Another edition. 1835.

Chap. v. The Cyrenaica and the Pentapolis.

Chap. vi. Tripoli and its immediate Dependencies.

172. ———— A German translation. Pesth, 1836-37. ' Gemälde der Berberie oder Geschichte und gegenwärtiger Zustand der Staaten Tunis, &c.'

173. 1830. **Gråberg de Hemsö.**—Carta dell' Africa.

See No. 109 of the Antologia.

174. 1830. **Treaty** between France and Tripoli, dated 11th Aug., negociated by Contre-Amiral de Rosamel, abolishing Christian slavery (which had already been abolished by Lord Exmouth in 1816), and generally regulating the relations between the two countries. Tab. des Etab. Fr. en Alg., 1841, p. 424. See also Tripoli Archives, No. 32.

175. 1832. **Papers** explanatory of the circumstances under which Sidi Hassuna D'Ghies has been accused by the Bashaw of Tripoli of having abstracted the papers of the late Major Laing. Blue Book. Folio, pp. 142.

176. 1832. **Shereef Mohamed Hassuna D'Ghies,** Late Minister to the Pacha of Tripoli.—A Statement to the Rt. Hon. Lord Goderich, Sec. of H.B.M. for the Colonies, concerning the expedition of the late Major Laing to Timbuctoo, and the affairs of Tripoli. Blue Book. Folio, pp. 54.

177. 1833. **Pouqueville.**—Mémoire historique et diplomatique sur le commerce et les établissements français au Levant, depuis l'an 500 de J. C. jusqu'à la fin du xvii siècle. Mém. de l'Inst. Roy. de France—Acad. des Inscr. et Bell. Lett. t. 10, p. 513.

This gives an interesting account of the origin of French consulates, and amongst others of those of Tripoli, Tunis, &c., in about 1617.

178. 1835. **Talma, A.**—Reistogtje langs en in eenige havens aan de Spaansche, Fransche, Italiansche en Barbarijsche kusten met de Nederlandsche korvet Dolfijn. Amsterdam : 8vo.

The portion treating of Tunis and Tripoli is from p. 88 to 101.

179. 1835. **Junker, P. S.**—Die Umschiffung Libyens durch die Phönizier. Conitz, 1835. Also Leipzig, 1841.

180. 1835. **Greenhow, Robert.**—Sketches of the history and present condition of Tripoli, with some accounts of the other Barbary States. The Southern Literary Messenger, Richmond, U.S.A., vol. i. p. 65, 128, 193, and vol. ii. 1, 69, 141, 213, 525, 669.

181. 1835. **Avezac, A. P. d'.**—Itinéraires dans l'intérieur de l'Afrique septentrionale, et discussion d'un nouveau canevas géodésique de cette région. Paris : 8vo.

This also appears as Relation d'un voyage dans l'intérieur d'Afrique septent. in the Bull. de la Soc. de Géog., 2 série, t. i. pp. 277 et seq.

182. 1836. ———— Études de Géographie critique sur une partie de l'Afrique septent. Itinéraires de Haggy-ebn-el-Dyn-el-Aghouathy, &c. Paris : 8vo, pp. viii. and 188, 1 map.

183. 1836. **Marcus, Louis.**—Histoire de Wandals .... accompagnée de recherches sur le commerce que les états barbaresques firent avec l'étranger. Paris : 8vo. 2nd edition, Paris, 1838. pp. 423 + 95.

The Vandals never extended their dominion beyond the sea-coast of Tripoli and the Cyrenaica.

184. 1836. **Karl Ritter.**—Géographie générale comparée, traduit de l'Allemand par P. Buret et Edouard Desor. Paris : 3 vol. 8vo.

Vol. iii. p. 210, contains an account of the Plateau of Barca and the Cyrenaica.

185. 1836. **Jaubert, Amédée.**—Géographie d'Edrisi traduit de l'Arabe en français, d'après deux MSS. de la Bibliothèque du Roi, et accompagnée de notes. T. i. 1836 ; t. ii. 1840.

Tripoli and Barca are mentioned at vol. i. pp. 252-285. The Arabic text and French translation were also published by Dozy and Goeje. Edrisi was born at Cueta in 1093.

See also Journ. Asiati. 3 ser. t. xi. p. 362.

186. 1836. **Delaporte, J. D.**, Consul de France à Tanger. Des Antiquités de de Leptis Magna. Journ. Asiatique, 3ᵉ ser. t. i. pp. 305-337.

Report written in 1806 to the Prince de Bénévent, Ministre des relations extérieures de l'Empire Français.

187. 1836. **Act of the British Parliament**, providing for Consular jurisdiction in .... Tripoli. Hertslet's Treaties, vol. v. p. 503.

188. 1837. **Ewald, Christn. Ferd.**—Reise von Tunis über Soliman, Nabal, Hammamet, Susa, Sfax, Gabis, Gerba nach Tripolis, und von da wieder zurück nach Tunis, im Jahre 1835. Herausgegeben von Paul Ewald, Nürenberg, Ebner, 1837-38. Large 8vo, 3 parts, 1 map, 8 black and 5 coloured engravings.

189. 1838. **Gibbon, Edward.**—The History of the Decline and Fall of the Roman Empire. London : 8vo, 12 vol.

Vol. iv. p. 286, chap. xxviii. The tyranny of Romanus in the Confederacy of Tripoli, A.D. 366.

Vol. viii. p. 227, chap. xlvi. The Greek colonies of Cyrene exterminated by Chosroes II., A.D. 614.

190. 1839. **Abou'l Féda, Ismael.** Description des pays du Maghreb. Texte Arab avec trad. par Ch. Solvat. Alger: 8vo, pp. 111-99.

191. 1839. **Walkenaer, Baron Ch. Atti.**—Rapport sur les recherches géographiques, historiques, archéologiques, qu'il conviendrait de continuer ou d'entreprendre dans l'Afrique septentrionale. Mém. de l'Inst. Acad. des Insc. et Bell. Lettres, t. xii. pp. 98-134. Also separately, Paris: 4to, pp. 83.

    At p. 106 he gives an account of previous explorations in the Cyrenaica and Tripoli.

192. 1839-1853. **Bocking, Edwardus.**—Notitia dignitatum et administrationum, omnium tam civilium quam militarum in partibus orientis et occidentis. Bonnae: 3 vol. (the last being an index), 8vo, pp. 540, 1009, 192. See also Rev. Afr. vol. vi. p. 135 et seq.

193. 1840. **Précis analytique** de l'histoire anc. d'Afrique septentrionale. See Tableau de la Situation des Établissements français for 1840. No. 195.

194. 1840. **Abou 'l Feda, Ismael.**—Texte Arabe publié d'après les Manuscrits de Paris et de Leyde aux frais de la Société Asiatique, par **M. Reinaud,** Membre de l'Institut, et le **Bn. MacGuckin de Slane.** Paris: 4to, pp. xlvii. 539.

195. 1841. **Ministère de la Guerre.**—Tableau de la Situation des Etablissements Français dans l'Algérie en 1840. Paris: 4to, pp. 452.

    In addition to much valuable information regarding Algeria before and after the Conquest, this volume contains a series of appendices of exceptional interest. The first three relate exclusively to Algeria. No. iv. is a " Précis analytique de l'histoire ancienne de l'Afrique Septentrionale " during the following periods : Carthaginian, Roman, Vandal, Byzantine; including an account of the introduction of Greek civilization into the Cyrenaica. No. v. " Division territoriale établie en Afrique par les Romans." No. vi. " Principaux traités de paix et de Commerce conclus par la France avec les Regences Barbaresques." No. vii. " Bibliographie Algerienne."

196. 1841. **Slane, le Baron MacGuckin de.**—Histoire de la province d'Afrique et des Maghrib, traduite de l'Arabe d'En-Noweiri. Journ. Asiat. 3 ser. tome xi. p. 97 et seq.

    This commences with the invasion of N. Africa by the Mohammedans in A.D. 647-8.

197. 1841. **Rotalier, Ch. de.** Histoire d'Alger et de la piraterie des Turcs dans la Méditerranée à dater du Seizième Siècle. Paris: 2 vol. pp. 447, 522.

    Tripoli taken by the Turks, vol. ii. p. 59.

198. 1841. **Ternaux-Compans, H.**—Bibliothèque Asiatique et Africaine, ou catalogue des ouvrages relatifs à l'Asie et à l'Afrique qui ont paru depuis la découverte de l'imprimerie jusqu'en 1750. Paris, Leipsick: 8vo, pp. 279.

    A most valuable work. Contains 2803 entries.

199. 1842. **Abou 'l Feda, Ismael.**—Géographie. Trad. Fr. par Reinaud et Guyard. Paris: 1842-1883, 2 vol. 4to.

200. 1842. **Slane, Baron MacGuckin de.**—Description de l'Afrique par **Ibn-Haucal.** Traduit de l'Arabe. Journ. Asiat. 3 ser. t. 13, pp. 153 and 209.

    The work commences with a description of the country between Barca and Gabes.

    Also Arab. text published by De Goeje, Leyden, 1871. English translation by Ousley, 1800.

201. 1842. **Mannert, Konrad.**—Géographie ancienne des États barbaresques. D'après l'Allemand de Mannert par L. Marcus et Duesberg, avec des additions et des notes par L. Marcus. Paris : 8vo, pp. 803.

Livre i. Libye ; Marmarique ; Cyrénaïque, &c. pp. 17-231.

202. 1844. **Strabo.**—Strabonis Rerum Geographicarum Libri XVII. Gr. et Lat. Oxonii : 2 vol. folio.

Many other editions.

An English edition of Strabo was published by H. G. Bohn in 1854-7, translated by H. C. Hamilton and W. Falconer. 3 vol. 12mo.

In Book xvii. c. iii. s. 18, is an account of the Syrtis and the Cyrenaica.

203. 1844. **Boeckh, Aug.**—Corpus Inscriptionum Graecarum, auctoritate et impensis Academiae Litterarum Regiae Borussicae, ab Materia collecta ab Augusto Boeckhio, edidit **Joannes Franzius.** Berolini : folio.

Vol. iii. fasc. i. part xxi., Inscriptiones Cyrenaicae.

This contains 237 Greek inscriptions from Cyrene, Ptolemais, Teuchira (Arsinoë), and Berenice.

204. 1844. **Avezac, A. P. d'.**—L'Univers : Esquisse Générale de l'Afrique, Aspect et Constitution physique, Histoire Naturelle, Ethnologie, Linguistique, État Social, Histoire, Explorations et Géographie. Paris : 8vo, pp. 272.

Première partie, La Libye propre, comprenant la Cyrénaïque et la Marmarique, pp. 67-157. Edifices de la Tripolitaine, p. 254.

Two illustrations of Cyrene.

205. 1844. **Zanoski, Jean.**—L'Univers, L'Afrique Chrétienne. Paris : 8vo, pp. 63.

206. ———— Histoire de la domination des Vandales en Afrique. Paris : 8vo, pp. 91.

207. ———— Histoire de l'Afrique sous la domination Byzantine, et appendices. Paris : 8vo, pp. 91, 102.

208. 1844. **Subtil, E.**—Sur les Mines de soufre de la Syrte. Rev. de l'Orient. t. v.

This paper, by the notorious sulphur explorer and adventurer of Tripoli, first induced Richardson to make his celebrated journey to the Sahara.

209. ———— Considérations politiques et commerciales sur Ghadames, suivies d'un Itinéraire de Tripoli à Ghadames. l. c. p. 97-123.

210. 1844. **De Slane, Baron MacGuckin.**—Sur les premiers expeditions des Musulmans en Mauritanie. Lettre à M. Hase, Membre de l'Institut. Paris : 8vo, pp. 39. Extract from Journ. Asiat. No. 9 of 1844.

Reply to M. Hase, who had asked the author if he could find in the writings of Arab authors exact information regarding the first expeditions of the Mohammedans in Africa. He gives a critical examination of En-Noweiri's work, the accuracy of which he disputes. He narrates on the authority of other authors the Arab invasion of the Cyrenaica and Tripoli in A.D. 641-644.

211. 1845. ———— Tripoli et Tunis. Considerations sur la possibilité d'une invasion des Turcs dans la Régence de Tunis par les frontières de Tripoli. Revue de l'Orient, vol. vii. pp. 281-286.

212. 1846. **Fresnel, F.** — Inscriptions Trilingues trouvées en May 1846 à Lebda (Leptis Magna).—Partie Punique avec la transcription Arabe. Journ. Asiat., 4th ser., vol. viii. pp. 349.

213. 1846. **Mackenzie, Alexander Slidell, U.S.N.**—The life of Stephen Decatur, a Commodore in the Navy of the U.S. Boston : 12mo, pp. 443.

This is contained in vol. xxi. of the Library of American Biography, conducted by Jared Sparks. Decatur's brilliant services on the Coast of Barbary are well known; he commanded the Philadelphia, which was captured by the Tripolitans. He subsquently recaptured and destroyed her.—See also N. Amer. Rev. vol. lxiv. pp. 27.

214. 1847. **Richardson, James.**—Touarick Alphabet, with the corresponding English and Arabic letters; Vocabularies of the Ghadamsee and Touarghee languages...with the 3rd Chapter of St. Matthew in the Ghadamsee and Kabail (or Algiers dialect) rendered (interlineally) into Latin by F. W. Newman, &c. London: folio.

215. 1847. **Khaldoun, Abou Zeid Abd-er-Rahman Ibn-Mohammed Ibn-,** Native and Magistrate of Tunis.—Histoire des Berbères et des Dynasties Muslemanes de l'Afrique septentrionale. Translation française par le **Baron MacGuckin de Slane.** Algiers: 4 vols.

The original work is a general history of the Mohammedan world, and is unsurpassed in Arabic literature as a masterpiece of historical composition. It was printed at Bulac, in 7 vols. royal 8vo, A.H. 1284. He was a native of Tunis; taught at Tlemçen; was first the captive and subsequently the friend of Timur, and died at Cairo in A.D. 1406.

At vol. i. p. 301 of de Slane's work are collected some of the most ancient Arab traditions regarding the first invasion of Africa by the Mohammedans, from a history of the conquest of Egypt by **Abd-er-Rahman ibn el-Hakim.** 1. "Conquête de Barca." 2. "Tripoli." At p. 313 are extracts from the great work of **En-Noweri** on the conquest of Africa, an account more detailed than that of Ibn-Khaldoun.

At vol. ii. p. 379 are extracts from **Ibn-el Ataîr.** "Les Siciliens attaquent la ville de Tripoli et détruisent celle de Djidjel." "Prise de Tripoli par les Francs," &c.

216. 1848. **Antoninus, Augustus.**—Itinerarium A. Augusti, ed. G. Parthey and M. Pinder. Berlin: 8vo.—See also Appendix to Shaw. No. 96.

217. 1848. **Orders of the Grand Vizier** to the Pasha of Tripoli for the repression of the Slave trade. Hertslet's Treaties, vol. ix. p. 738.

218. 1848. **Vizirial Letter** to the Pasha of Tripoli prohibiting the Slave Trade. Hertslet's Treaties, vol. xiii. p. 836.

219. 1848. **Richardson, James.**—Travels in the Great Desert of Sahara, in the years 1845–46, containing a narrative of personal adventures during a tour of nine months through the desert, amongst the Touaricks and other tribes of Saharan peoples. Including a description of the oases and cities of Ghat, Ghadames and Mourzouk. London: 2 vol. 8vo, pp. 440, 482, with map and numerous illustrations.

The author started from Tripoli and returned to the coast at Mesrata, having made a journey of 1600 miles.

220. 1848. **MacCarthy, O.**—Voyage dans le grand désert de Sahara en 1845–46 par James Richardson. Rev. de l'Orient, de l'Alg. et des Colon. t. 3, pp. 127–136.

221. 1848. **Bourville, J. Vattier de.**—Lettre à M. Letronne sur les premiers résultats de son voyage à Cyrène. Rev. Arch. t. v. p. 150.

222. 1848. **Letronne, J. Ant.**—Quelques notes sur la lettre de M. de Bourville relative à l'exploration de la Cyrénaïque. Rev. Arch. t. v. p. 279.

223. —— Deux nouvelles inscriptions Grecques de la Cyrénaïque véritable emplacement de Cyrène. l. c. p. 432.—See also Journ. des Savants, pp. 370-377. These were found by M. Vattier de Bourville.

224. 1848. **Lenormant, Ch.**—Note sur un Vase Panathénaïque récemment découvert à Bengazi, lue à l'Académie des Inscr. et Bell. Lett. 30 Juin. Rev. Arch. t. v. p. 230.

225. 1849. **Fresnel, Fulgence,** French Consul at Djedda. Mémoire sur le Waday. Bull. Soc. Géogr. Paris, 3 ser. t. 11. pp. 6 to 14.

This paper gives much valuable and original information on the commerce between Waday and the seaports of Bengazi and Tripoli. Corrections and additions to this memoir were published in the following volume; p. 356. It is continued l. c., t. xiii. pp. 82, 341 ; t. xiv. pp. 153-315.

226. 1849. **Barth, H.**—Wanderungen durch die Küstenländer des Mittelmeeres, Ausgeführt in den Jahren 1845-1847. Berlin: 8vo.

227. 1850. **Jomard.**—Instructions pour le voyage de M. Prax dans le Sahara Septentrional. Mém. de l'Inst. Acad. Inscr. et Bell. Lett. t. xvi. pp. 54-68.

At p. 62 are suggestions relative to the Cyrenaica, &c.

228. —— Instructions à M. Vattier de Bourville pour l'exploration de la Cyrénaïque, l. c., pp. 68-84.

229. 1850. **Bourville, M. Vattier de.**—Rapport sur les premières fouilles opérées à Benghazi. l. c., p. 91.

230. 1850. **Prax, Lieut. de Vaisseau.**—Régence de Tripoli. Rev. de l'Orient. de l'Algérie et des Colonies (Bull. de la Soc. Orient. in succession to the Rev. de l'Orient), t. vii. pp. 257-280 et seq.

From information obtained at second hand.

231. —— Carte de la Régence de Tripoli, et des principales routes commerciales de l'Intérieur de l'Afrique. Bull. Soc. Géogr. Paris : 3 ser. t. xiv. p. 81.

233. 1850. **Richardson, J.**—Routes of the Sahara. Itinéraires dans l'Intérieur du Grand Désert d'Afrique par . . . Traduit de l'Anglais par M. Albert-Montémont, membre de la Commission Centrale. (Extrait du rapport fait au Foreign Office en 1845-46, par M. Richardson.) Bull. Soc. Géogr. Paris, 3 ser. t. xiii. p. 73, t. xiv. pp. 104-203, 380.

234. 1850. **Testa, E.**—Aanteekeningen wegens de Verkenning, het inkomen en de aukerplaats van de Haven van Tripoli in Barbarye en de winden en stroomen, welke aldaar heerschen volgens plaatselijke waarnemingen verzameld. Amsterdam : 8vo, pp. 82.

235. 1850. **Hoefer, Dr. Fred.**—États Tripolitains. Paris : 8vo, pp. 128.

Two illustrations, one being the Quadrifrontal Arch. From "L'Univers: Histoire et description de tous les peuples."

236. 1850. **Orders of the Grand Vizier** to the Pasha of Tripoli for the repression of the Slave Trade. Hertslet's Treaties, vol. ix. p. 739.

237. 1851. **American Diplomacy** with the Barbary powers. Their piracies and aggressions. Amer. Whig Rev. new ser. vol. ii. (whole coll. xiii.) pp. 27-33.

238. 1852. **Cherbonneau.**—Voyage du Cheikh Ibn-Batuta à travers l'Afrique Septentrionale au commencement du xiv⁰ Siècle. Tiré de l'original Arabe et accompagné de Notes. Paris : 8vo, pp. 88. Reprinted from Nouv. Ann. des Voy. An abstract of Ibn Batuta's great work q. v.

239. 1853. **Ibn Batuta,** Voyages d'.—Texte arabe, accompagné d'une traduction par **C. Defrémery** et le **Dr. B. R. Sanguinetti.** Paris: 4 vol. 8vo, published by the Société Asiatique.

Vol. i. p. 26. The author arrives at Tripoli on his outward journey.

240. 1853. **Rousseau, Alphonse.**—Voyage du Scheikh Et-Tidjani dans la Régence de Tunis. (1306–1309.) Rev. Asiat. ser. v. t. i. p. 102.

This portion of the work contains a history of Tripoli. See page 141.

241. 1853. **Sumner, Charles.**—White Slavery in the Barbary States. London: 8vo, pp. 135.

This contains a notice of the American war with Tripoli. The first edition was published in the U.S. in 1847.

242. 1853. **Richardson, James.**—Narrative of a Mission to Central Africa performed in the years 1850–51 under the orders and at the expense of H.M. Government. Edited by Bayle St. John. London: 2 vol. 8vo, pp. 343, 359, with outline map.

Richardson started from Tripoli; he visited Mourzouk, Ghat, Aghadez, Damerghou, and thence East to Ungurutua, six days' march from Kuka, where he died on the 4th March, 1851.

243. 1854. **Petermann, Augustus.**—An account of the progress of the expedition to Central Africa, performed by order of H.M. Foreign Office, under Messrs. Richardson, Barth, Overweg and Vogel, in the years 1850–51–52–53, consisting of maps and illustrations with descriptive notes, constructed and compiled from private materials. London: folio, pp. 14, 3 maps.

244. 1854. **Smyth, William Henry,** Rear-Admiral.—The Mediterranean: A Memoir, Physical, Historical and Nautical. London: 8vo, pp. 519.

At pp. 85–90 is a description of the Coasts of the Cyrenaica and Tripoli.

245. 1855. **Order of the Porte** to the Pasha of Tripoli for preventing the traffic in slaves from Tripoli to Candia. Hertslet's Treaties, vol. x. p. 602.

246. ——— Vizerial letter on the same subject. l. c., vol. xiii. p. 837.

247. 1855. **Dinomé, l'Abbé.**—Coup d'œil rapide sur les informations obtenues depuis la fin du xviii° siècle au sujet de l'intérieur de l'Afrique Septentrionale. Orleans: 8vo.

248. 1855. **Pliny.**—The Natural History of Pliny, translated by Bostock and Riley. Bohn's Classical Library, London: 8vo.

In Book v. is an account of the Syrtes and the Cyrenaica.

249. 1855. **Pellissier de Reynaud, E.**—La Régence de Tripoli. Rev. des Deux Mondes, vol. xii. p. 1.

An excellent account of the Regency, with notices of the various expeditions that had been undertaken in and from it.

250. 1855. **Vogel, Dr. Eduard.**—Reise nach Central-Afrika. Erster Abschnitt; Reise von Tripoli (Durch Tripolitanien, Fessan, Das land der Teda) bis zum Tsad-see, März 1853—Januar 1854. Nach den Original-Documenten, vom Herausgeber. Petermann, Geogr. Mitth. pp. 237–259, with map (that of Richardson, Barth, Overweg and Vogel).

251. 1855. **Barth, Dr. Heinrich.**—Reisen und Entdeckungen in Nord- und Central-Afrika, in den Jahren 1850–1851–1852, 1853, 1854 und 1855. Mit Karten und Holzschnitten. Petermann, Geogr. Mitth. pp. 306–310.—See also l. c., pp. 230, 267.

252. 1856. **Report of the Governor of Tripoli** relative to the prevention of Slave Trade. Hertslet's Treaties, vol. x. p. 1011.

253. 1856. **Testa, Le Ch. E.**, Dutch Consul-General in Tripoli. Notice Statistique et Commerciale sur la Régence de Tripoli de Barbarie. La Haye: 8vo, pp. 34.

The author resided 10 years in Tripoli.

254. 1856. **Malte-Brun, V. A.**—Résumé Historique de la grande exploration de l'Afrique Centrale faite de 1850 à 1855, par J. Richardson, H. Barth, A. Overweg, avec une carte itinéraire. Paris: 8vo, pp. 108.

255. 1856. **Hamilton, James.**—Wanderings in North Africa. London: 8vo, pp. 320, 8 illustrations, all of ruins, &c. in the Cyrenaica.

The author started from Bengazi, visited Cyrene, Derna, Ptolemeita, Teucra, and back to Bengazi; thence eastwards by Angila to Jupiter Ammon, and so to Egypt.

256. 1857. **Barth, Dr. Heinrich.**—Reisen und Entdeckungen in Nord- und Central-Afrika in den Jahren 1849 bis 1855, von H. B. Tagebuch seiner in Auftrag der Brittischen Regierung unternommenen Reise. Mit Karten, Holzschnitten, und Bildern. Gotha: 8vo, 5 Bde.

An English translation of this work, 'Travels and Discoveries in North and Central Africa, being a Journal of an Expedition undertaken under the auspices of H.M. Government in the years 1848-1855.'' London: 8 vol. 8vo, with many maps and illustrations.

See also Précis des resultats et des informations obtenus par le Dr. B. dans ses Voyages dans l'interieur de l'Afrique ; analyse du V°. vol. et resumé général par l'Abbé Dinomé. Nouv. Ann. des Voy. July, 1859.

257. —— Die Imosch ark oder Tuareg, Volk und Land. Peterm. Geogr. Mitth. p. 239, plate 11.—See also ' Tour de Monde,' 1866, p. 193 et seq.

The portions of Dr. Barth's work treating of the Tripolitaine are vol. i. pp. 1-181 and vol. v. pp. 441-453.

258. 1857. **Macé, Ant. P. Laur.**—Des Voyageurs Modernes dans la Cyrénaïque et le Silphium des Anciens. Paris: 8vo.

259. 1857. **Fournel, Mar. Jér. H.**, Ingénieur des Mines.—Étude sur la conquête d'Afrique par les Arabes: et recherches sur les tribus berbères qui ont occupé le Magreb central. Paris: 4to, pp. 165.

260. —— Les Berbers, étude sur la conquête de l'Afrique par les Arabes, d'après les textes imprimés. Paris: n. d., 4to.

Both works of considerable importance.

261. 1857. **Een dag te Tripoli.**—Fragment uit dagboek van een zee-officier. Amsterdam, 8vo, pp. 423.

262. 1857. **Orenz, K.**—Die Entdeckungsreisen in Nord- und Mittel-Afrika von Richardson, Overweg, Barth, und Vogel. Leipzig : with map.

263. 1858. **Gottschick, A. F.**, Director des Königl. Pädagogiums zu Putbus.—Geschichte der Gründung und Blüthe des hellenischen Staates in Kyrenaika. Leipzig: 8vo, pp. 40.

264. 1858. **Tripoli.**—Sharpe's London Mag., new ser. vol. xiii. pp. 84-87.

An account of the Regency and the various explorations that had been made in it.

265. 1858. **Vizirial Letter** to the Pasha of Tripoli prohibiting the Slave Trade. Hertslet's Treaties, vol. xiii. p. 837.

266. 1858–60.   **Rawlinson, George,** assisted by **Sir Henry Rawlinson** and **Sir J. G. G. Wilkinson.**—The History of Herodotus. A new English version, with copious notes and appendices. London: 8vo, 4 vols.

References to Barca; ii. 483, iii. 138, 179. Cyrene, iii. 134, 135, 149, 171. Syrtes, iii. 148. Oea, iii. 291.

Copious notes, with illustrations, regarding the Cyrenaica at vol. iii. p. 132.

267. 1859.   **El-Bekri.**   Description de l'Afrique Septentrionale, traduit par **Mac Guckin de Slane.** Paris: 8vo, pp. 432.

A description of Tripoli and the Cyrenaica, from p. 11 to p. 44.

268. 1859.   **Berbrugger, A.**—Domination Romaine dans le Sud de l'Afrique Septentrionale—Tripolitaine, d'après le Dr. Barth. Rev. Afr. vol. iii. pp. 379–390.

269. 1859.   **Schauenberg, Dr. Ed.**—Reisen in Central-Afrika. Zweiter Band. I. Richardson, II. Barth, Ad. Overweg, E. Vogel. Lahr: 8vo, pp. 566, with a map of all the expeditions starting southward from Tripoli.

270. 1860.   **Headley, J. T.**—Eaton's Barbary Expedition. Harp. New Month. Maga. vol. xxi. pp. 496–511.

A very full account of this remarkable enterprise.

271. 1860.   **Duveyrier, Henri.**—Notes sur la régence de Tripoli. Rev. Alg. et Colon. December.

The author says of this that it was a "simple lettre qui n'était pas destinée à l'impression."

272. 1860.   **Heine, Wilhelm.**—Eine Sommerreise nach Tripolis. Berlin: 12mo, pp. 322.

273. 1860.   **Muller, L.**—Numismatique de l'Ancienne Afrique—ouvrage préparé et commencé par **C. T. Falbe** et **J. Chr. Lindberg.** Refait, achevé et publié par L. Müller. Copenhague: 3 vol. 4to, and supplement.

Vol. i.—Les Monnaies de la Cyrénaïque.   pp. xii. 174.

Vol. ii.—Les Monnaies de la Syrtique, de la Byzacène et la Zeugitane. pp. viii. 188.

Vol. viii.—Les Monnaies de la Numidie et de la Mauritanie.   pp. vi. 194.

Supplement.   Additional coins from all these regions.   pp. iv. 96.

All profusely illustrated.   A standard work.

274. 1861.   **El-Ya'goubi.**—Descriptio al Maghribi. Leyden: Arab-Latin, 8vo.

275. ——   Specimen e literis orientalibus exhibens Kitabi' l-Boldan, sive librum Regionum auctore Ahmed ibn Abi Yaqub, noto nomine Al-Yaqubi quem auspice viro clarissimo **T. G. J. Juynboll** nunc primum Arabice edidit **Abramus Wilhelmus T. Juynboll.** Lugduni-Batavorum: 8vo, pp. 154.

276. 1861.   **Krafft-Krafftshagen, Alexander Freiherrn von** (Hadji Scander).—Tripolis und die Städte der kleinen Syrte. Peterm. Geogr. Mitth. pp. 199.

277. ——   Promenades dans la Tripolitaine, 1860. Tour de Monde, vol. iii. pp. 66–80, with map and numerous illustrations.

The author travelled as a Mohammedan pilgrim.

278. ——   Les Villes de la Tripolitaine. Rev. Arch. Paris, Nouv. Sér., vol. iv. pp. 29.

279. 1861.   **Vivien de Saint-Martin.**—Sur les anciens cités de la Tripolitaine. Lue à l'Académie des Inscriptions et Belles-Lettres dans la Séance du 13 Sep. A review of Baron de Krafft's paper last before quoted, and his communication to the Tour de Monde. No. 57, t. iii. 1861, p. 66.

280. 1861. **Laval.**—Topographie Médicale de la ville de Derna, ancienne Cyrénaïque. Gaz. Méd. d'Orient. Constantinople, t. iv. pp. 5-15.

281. 1861. **Duveyrier, Henri.**—Statistique du Djebel Nefoûsa, Montagnes de la Régence de Tripoli. Nouv. Ann. des Voy. August.

282. —— Relations commerciales de Ghadames (Régence de Tripoli) avec le Soudan. Ann. du Commerce extérieur, No. 1346. June.

283. —— Reisen und Forschungen im Grenzgebiete von Algier, Tunis und Tripoli. 1860 (Nebst einer Originalkarte), Peterm. Geogr. Mitth. 1861, p. 389, map 13.

284. 1862. **Beurmann.**—Brief des Herrn Maritz von Beurmann an Herrn Dr. H. Barth. Murzuk 27th April. Zeitsch. für Allgem. Erdkunde, vol. xiii. pp. 44.

285. —— Brief des Herrn M. von Beurmann an Herrn Dr. H. Barth. Ueber einem Ausflug in das Wadi Scherki und seine Abreise nach Bornu. (Hierzu eine Karte Taf. iv.) l. c., pp. 347.

286. —— Einige Bemerkungen von Dr. H. Barthe zu Herrn v. Beurmann's Kartenskizzen aus Fessan und Barka. l. c., pp. 352.

287. 1862. **Grad, Charles.**—Edouard Vogel, et son exploration de l'Afrique Centrale. Bull. Soc. Geogr. Paris, p. 77.

This is a biographical sketch of Vogel from his birth in 1829 till his murder in 1856, based on his letters and memoirs, published in Peterman's Mitth. and in the Proceedings of the R.G.S.

288. 1862. **Vaux, W. S. W.**—An account of the recent excavations at Cyrene by Lt. R. M. Smith R.E., and Lt. Porcher, R.N. Proceed. Soc. Antiq. Second Ser. vol. ii. p. 96. Also Trans. Roy. Soc. of Liter. vol. vii.

289. 1862. **The Cyrenian Marbles.**—Art Journal, New Series, vol. i. p. 20. An account of the antiquities sent home by Lieuts. Smith and Porcher to the British Museum.

290. 1862. **Reade, Vice-Consul.**—Report on the trade of Tripoli for 1861. Consular Comm. Reports, 1862, p. 336.

291. 1862. **Aquilina, Vice-Consul.**—Report on the trade of Bengasi for 1861. l. c. p. 339.

292. 1862. **De Tremaux, Vice-Consul.**—Report on the trade of Derna for 1861. l. c. p. 341.

293. 1862. **Vivien de Saint-Martin.**—Ueber die Lage der alten Städte von Tripolitanien. Vortrag, gehalten am 13 Sep. 1861 in der Académie des Inscriptions et Belles-Lettres. Peterm. Geogr. Mitth. p. 11, plate 3.

294. 1862. **Tauxier, H.**—Examen des traditions grecques, latines et musulmanes, relatives à l'origine du peuple berbère, l. c., pp. 353 et seq.

A résumé of this, under the title ' Études sur les Migrations des nations berbères,' is given in the Journal Asiat., Oct., pp. 340-54. The writer takes as his point of departure the distribution of Berber tribes at the time of the Arab invasion, and the base of his investigations is of course the celebrated work of Ibn Khaldoun.

296. 1863. **Reade, Vice-Consul.**—Report on the trade of Bengasi for 1862. Consular Comm. Reports, p. 439.

297. 1863. **De Tremaux, Vice-Consul.**—Report on the trade of Derna for 1862. l. c., p. 440.

298. 1863. **Herman, Consul-General.**—Report on the trade of Tripoli for 1862. l. c., p. 441.

299. 1863. **Guys, Charles Edouard**, ancien consul.—Notice sur les îles de Bomba, et Plate, le Golfe de Bomba et ses environs avec la relation d'un voyage sur la côte de l'est et celle de l'ouest de la Régence Tripolitaine. Marseille : 8vo, pp. 56.

300. 1863. **Grad, Charles.**—Les Expeditions Allemandes à la recherche d'Edouard Vogel. Nouv. Ann. des Voy., May and June.

301. 1863. **Tauxier, H.**—Ethnographie de l'Afrique septentrionale au temps de Mahomet. Rev. Afr. vol. vii. p. 453.

302. 1863. **Duveyrier, Henri.**—Les Touâreg du Nord. Paris : 8vo., pp. xxxiv.· 499, and Supp. pp. 37, Map and xxv. Plates.

A very important work for which the Geographical Society of Paris awarded its Gold Medal. M. Duveyrier started from Constantine in 1859, proceeded to the country of the Beni M'Zab, thence to El Golea and other parts of the Algerian Sahara. He subsequently explored the Tunisian Sahara, Ghadames, Rhat, Mourzouk, and Zouila, reaching Tripoli by the long route of the Sokna. The journey lasted during three years. In a first appendix the author treats of the ancient geography of the country. In a separate appendix, M. Bourguignat describes the Mollusca observed, with 3 plates, and M. Cosson the new plants, 3 plates.

303. 1863. **Amari.**—I Diplomi arabi del reale archivio Fiorentino. Firenze : 4to.

This valuable work contains, amongst others, 41 documents connected with Florentine relations with Tripoli and the other Barbary States.

304. 1863. **Mission de Ghadamès.**—Septembre, Octobre, Novembre, et Decembre, 1862. Rapports officiels et documents à l'appui. Alger : 8vo, pp. 358, with numerous illustrations.

This mission was sent by the Governor-General of Algeria, and was commanded by **Colonel Mircher.** With him were associated Capitaine de Polignac, l'Ingénieur Vatonne, l'Aide-Major Hoffman and the Interpreter Ismael bou Derba. Its object was to open commercial relations with the great markets of the Soudan. It went by sea to Tripoli, and thence to Ghadamès by El-Oued. See also Rev. des deux Monde and Bull. Soc. Géogr. Paris, 2ᵉ Sem. p. 405.

305. 1863. **Vivien de Saint-Martin.**—Le Nord de l'Afrique dans l'antiquité Grecque et Romaine, Étude Historique et Géographique. Ouvrage couronné en 1860 par l'Académie des Inscription et Belles-Lettres. With 4 maps. Paris : 8vo, pp. xx. 519.

Section ii. L'Afrique d'Hérodote, Art. ii. s. 3. Les tribus de la région littorale depuis la frontière d'Egypte jusqu'à l'entrée du territoire Carthaginois. —See also Petermann, Geogr. Mitth. 1862, p. 11 ; Jour. des Sav. p. 398.

306. 1863. **Petermann, A., und B. Hassenstein.**—Inner-Afrika, nach dem Stande der Geographischen Kentniss in den Jahren 1861 bis 1863. Gotha : 4to, pp. 164, with 10 sections of their great map of Africa.

The first only refers to Fezzan.

307. 1864. **Rousseau, Alphonse, Consul de France.**—Annales Tunisiennes. Alger : 8vo, pp. 571.

At p. 88 is an allusion to the siege of Tripoli by the Tunisians, and to the plague of 1708.

308. 1864. **De Champlouis, M. Nau**, Capitaine au Corps Impérial d'État-major.—Notice sur la carte de l'Afrique sous la domination des Romains, dressée au Dépôt de la Guerre d'après les travaux de **M. Fr. Lacroix,** par ordre de S.E. le Maréchal Comte Randon, Min. de la Guerre. Paris : 4to, pp. 46.

The map in question is in two large sheets (2,000,000°), and includes the whole district between the Cyrenaica and the Atlantic. See also L'Ann. Géogr., t. iii. p. 110.

309. 1864. **Mas Latrie, Le Comte L.** de.—L'Afrique sous la domination des Romains. Paris.

310. 1864. **Smith, Capt. R. Murdoch, R.E.,** and **Commander E. A. Porcher, R.N.**—History of the recent discoveries at Cyrene, made during an expedition to the Cyrenaica in 1860-1861, under the auspices of H.M. Government. London : Imp. 4to, pp. 98.

Superbly illustrated, with 12 maps and plans, 22 plates in double-tinted lithography, 16 photographs, 10 plates of Greek inscriptions, and 26 woodcuts.

311. 1864. **Reade, Vice-Consul.**—Report on the trade of Bengasi for the half-year ending 30th Nov. 1863. Cons. Comm. Reports, p. 407.

312. ———— Do. for the year ending 31st Dec. 1863. l. c., p. 408.

313. 1864. **De Tremaux, Vice-Consul,** on the trade of Derna for 1863. l. c., p. 410.

314. 1864. **Herman, Consul-General,** on the trade of Tripoli for 1863. l. c., p. 411.

315. 1864. **Sprenger, Aloys.**—Two letters from Africa regarding the murder of Ed. Vogel. Zeitsch. des Morgenland Gesellsch. t. xvii. No. 2, April.

316. ———— On the death of Madlle. Tinné and the botanist H. Schubet. l. c., August.

317. 1864. **Grad, Charles.**—Les expéditions Allemandes à la recherche l'Edouard Vogel de 1861 à 1862 ; d'Après des lettres et des Mémoires originaux des Membres de la Mission. Nouv. Ann. des Voy., Novembre.

318. 1864. **Petermann, A.**—Neue Karte vom Mittelländischen Meer u. Nord-Afrika. Peterm. Geogr. Mitth. pp. 182, 191.

319. 1865. **Rohlfs, Gerhard.**—Nachrichten von Gerhard Rohlfs aus Tripoli. Petermann, Geogr. Meitth., p. 235.

320. ———— Ausflug von Tripoli nach Lebda. l. c., p. 263.

321. ———— Nachrichten von Gerhard Rohlfs aus Rhadames. l. c., p. 305.

322. ———— Tagebuch seiner Reise durch Marokko nach Tuat. 1864. 1. Abschnitt : Reise von Tanger bis Ued-Sidi-Hassan, 14 März bis 9 Mai 1864. l. c., p. 82, map 4. 2. Abschnitt : Reise von Uled-Sidi-Hassan bis Karsas im Ued Ssaura, 10 Mai bis 25 Juli. l. c., p. 165, map 6. 3. Abschnitt : Reise von Karsas im Ued Ssaura nach ain Salah, 29 Juli bis 17 September, und allgemeine Beschreibung von Tuat. l. c., p. 402, map 14, and 1886, p. 119.

323. 1865. **Primaudaie, Elie de la.**—Le littoral de la Tripolitaine : Commerce, navigation, géographie comparée. Paris : 8vo, pp. 200, with map.

From Nouv. Annales des Voyages, July, August, and September.

324. 1865. **Walker, Acting Cons. Gen.**—Report on the trade of Tripoli for 1864. Cons. Comm. Rep., p. 125.

325. 1865. **Dennis, Vice-Consul.**—Report on the trade of Bengazi for 1864, l. c., p. 660. A full and excellent report.

326. 1866. **Mas Latrie, Comte L. de,** Chef de Section aux Archives.—Traités de Paix et de Commerce et documents divers concernant les relations des Chrétiens avec les Arabes de l'Afrique Septentrionale au moyen âge. Paris : 4to, pp. xxvii. 342 + 402 + 118.
A work of the highest value. It contains—1. A preface ; 2. A historical introduction ; 3. Documents regarding Christian relations with the Arabs ; 4. Supplementary documents.

327. 1866. **Barth, H.**— Sammlung und Bearbeitung Central-Afrikanischer Vokabularien. 3 Abth. Nennwörter. 4to, pp. 143-295.

328. 1866. **Rohlfs, Gerhard.**—Neueste Briefe von G. R. und Rückblick auf seine bisherigen Reisen in Afrika in den Jahren 1861 bis 1865. Peterm. Geogr. Mitth. p. 3, plate 2.

329. ——— Tagebuch seiner Reise von Tuat nach Rhadames, 1864. l. c., p. 8.

330. ——— Nachrichten von Gerhard Rohlfs aus Mursuk. l. c., pp. 118-227.

331. ——— Briefe von G. R. aus Bilma, Mai und Juni 1866. l. c., pp. 356-368.

332. ——— Account of a Journey across the Atlas Mountains and through the Oases Tuat and Tidikelt to Tripoli by way of Ghadames in the year 1864. Proc. R. Geogr. Soc., Lond., vol. ix. No. vi. pp. 312-314.

333. 1866. **Hassenstein, B.**—Mémoire zur Karte von G. Rohlfs Reise durch die Oasen von Tuat und Tidikelt, 1864. Nebst Bericht über Major Laing's Reise 1825 und Duveyrier's Erkundigungen in Nord-Africa. Peterm. Géogr. Mitth. p. 53. For the map in question see l. c. 1865, No. 14.

334. 1866. **Kunth, A.**—Ueber die von Gerhard Rohlfs auf Reise von Tripoli nach Ghadames im Mai und Juni 1865, gefundenen Versteinerungen. Zeitschr. der Gesell. für Erdk. zu Berlin, heft iv. pp. 319-323, with map.

335. 1866. **Dennis, Vice-Consul.**—Report on the trade of Bengazi for 1865. Cons. Comm. Reports, p. 501.

336. 1866. **Drummond Hay, Cons.-Gen. Frank.**—Report on the trade of Tripoli for 1865. l. c., p. 497.

337. 1867. **Rohlfs, Gerhard.**—Uebersicht von G. R. Reise durch Afrika, 1866 bis 1867. Peterm. Geogr. Mitth. p. 372, map 12.

338. ——— Reise durch Marokko, Uebersteigung des Grossen Atlas. Exploration der Oasen von Tafilet, Tuat und Tidikelt und Reise durch die Grosse Wüste über Rhadames nach Tripoli. Bremen : 8vo, pp. 207, with map.

339. ——— Résumé de Voyage de Gerhard R. de Tripoli à Lagos, d'Après les Mitth. du Dr. Petermann, lib. x. p. 372, 1867. Bull. Soc. Géogr. Paris, 5e ser. t. 14, p. 395.

340. 1867. **Drummond-Hay, Cons.-Gen. Frank.**—Report on the trade of Tripoli for 1866. Cons. Comm. Reports, part i. p. 134, and part ii. p. 110.

341. 1867. **Dennis, Vice-Consul.**—Report on the trade of Bengazi for 1866. l. c., part ii. p. 113.

342. 1868. **Brine, Lindesay,** Commander R.N.—On the past and present inhabitants of the Cyrenaica. 88th Meeting of Brit. Ass. Norwich. Notices and Abstracts, p. 181.
A short abstract of the author's visit to that part of the coast between Berenice and the Egyptian frontier in 1867.

343. 1868. **Rohlfs, Gerhard.**—Reise durch Nord-Afrika vom Mittelländischen Meere bis zum Busen von Guinea, 1865-1867. 1. Hälfte; von Tripoli nach Kuka (Fesan, Sahara, Bornu). Gotha : 4to, pp. 75, 2 maps.

344. 1868. **Beulé.**—Découvertes à Cyrène. Journ. des Savants, pp. 273-291. A review of Smith and Porcher's work.

345. 1869. **Drummond-Hay, Cons.-Gen. Frank.**—Report on the trade of Tripoli for 1868. Cons. Comm. Reports, p. 525.

346. 1869. **Vizirial Letter** to the Governor General of Tripoli relative to the prohibition of the Slave Trade. Hertslet's Treaties, vol. xiii. p. 837.

347. 1869. **Chaunebot, A.** Empire Ottoman. Esquisse d'un projet de Colonisation de la Cyrénaïque. Paris : 8vo, pp. 43.

348. 1869. **Bompois, Ferdinand.**—Médailles Grecques autonomes frappées dans la Cyrénaïque. Notice accompagnée d'explications nouvelles sur différents points de numismatique et d'antiquité. Paris : 8vo, pp. 123, pl. 3.
Published at the office of the Revue Numismatique.

349. 1869. **Rohlfs, Gerhard.**—Leptis Magna. Sabratha. Das Ausland, No. 20, pp. 473-477; No. 22, pp. 522-526.

350. —— Rapport sur le Voyage de Bengasi à l'Oasis de Jupiter-Ammon, par les Oasis d'Audjila et Djalo. Bull. Soc. Géogr. Paris, June, pp. 465-471.

351. —— Berenice, Die Hesperiden-Gärten und der Letha-Fluss. Die Jupiter-Ammons-Oase. Das Ausland, No. 41, pp. 969-971; No. 42, pp. 985-989; No. 43, pp. 347-352.

352. —— Bengasi. l. c., No. 40, pp. 947-952.

353. —— Audjila und Djalo. l. c., No. 49, pp. 1153-1158.

354. 1869. **Cyrène.**—Article in Larousse, Grand Dict. Univ. du xixᵉ Siècle, t. v. p. 731.

355. 1869. **Kanitz, A.**—Auszug aus Plantae Tinneanae. Vindobonae : 1867. Text mit Nachträgen. Berlin : 8vo.

356. 1869. **Belin, M.** Bibliographie Ottomane. Journ. Asiat., ser. vi. t. xiv. p. 71.
Amongst works published at Constantinople is the following :—

طرابلوس غرب تاريخي. Histoire de Tripolie de Barbarie.

Mehemmed Bebidjeddin efendi, great-grandson of the Cheikh el-Islam Aâchir efendi, who had translated into Turkish the Arabic history of Abou Abd-Allah Mohammed ibn Khalil Ghalboun Taratoucy.

357. 1870. **Rohlfs, Gerhard.**—Land und Volk in Afrika. Bericht aus den Jahren 1865 bis 1870. Bremen : 8vo, pp. 240.

358. —— Zur Karte von Cyrenaica. Mit 1 Karte. Zeitsch. der Gesell. für Erdk. zu Berlin. 5 Bund. 4 Heft. pp. 370.

359. 1870. **Nachtigal, Dr.** — Relation de la mort de Mademoiselle Alexina Tinné, et voyage au Tibesti. Lettre à M. Henri Duveyrier ; dated Mourzouk, 2nd Dec. 1869. Bull. Soc. Géogr. Paris, 5 sér. t. xix. p. 89.
Dr. Nachtigal and Mademoiselle Tinné left Mourzouk together, the former for Bournou, the latter for Tibesti. She was killed, and her caravan pillaged by the Touaregs, no doubt from cupidity. This letter is followed by observations by M. H. Duveyrier, and by an account of Nachtigal's journey to Tibesti.

360. 1870. **Nachtigal, Dr.**—Reise Dr. G. N——'s nach Tibesti aus brieflichen Mittheilungen. Schreiben Dr. N——'s an Dr. A. Bastian. Mit 1 Karte. Zeitschr. Gesell. für Erdk. zu Berlin: 5 Bd. 1 Heft, pp. 69–75.

361. —— Briefe des Herrn Dr. —— an Herrn Dr. A. Bastian. l. c., 3 Heft. pp. 265–269.

362. —— Die Tibbu. Ethnographische Skizze. l. c., 5 Bd. pp. 216–242.

363. 1870. **Zurcher et Margolle, MM.**—Mademoiselle Tinné, 1861–69. Le Tour du Monde, No. 566, pp. 289–304.

A Biography of Mademoiselle Tinné, and an account of her murder near Mourzouk.

364. 1870. **Segni, P. Philippe da.**—Viaggio da Tripoli di Barbaria al Bornou nel 1850. Boll. della Soc. Geogr. ital., Fasc. 4, pp. 137–150.

365. 1870. **Wiet, E.**—La Tripolitaine. Bull. Soc. Géogr. Paris, July to Dec., 5 ser. t. xx. pp. 175–193.

Communicated by the Ministère des Affaires Étrangères. This includes an account of Bengazi, Tolemeïta, Derna, Bomba and Tobrouk.

366. 1870. **Dennis, George.**—On recent excavations in the Greek Cemeteries of the Cyrenaica. Trans. Royal Soc. of Lit., 2 ser. vol. ix. pp. 135–182, with 4 illustrations.

A valuable paper, though the author describes his experience as "a tale of fruitless labours and repeated disappointments."

367. 1870. **Maltzan, Heinrich, Freiherrn von.**—Reise in den Regentschaften Tunis und Tripolis. Nebst einem Anhang: Ueber die neuentdeckten phönicischen Inschriften von Karthago. Mit Titelkupfer, Plan von Tunis und 59 lithographirten Inschriften. Leipzig: 8vo, 3 vol. pp. 401, 436, 386.

The third volume is devoted to Tripoli.

368. 1871. **Die Wehrkraft** des Osmanischen Reiches und seiner Vasallen-Staaten Egypten, Tunis und Tripolis. Wien: 8vo, pp. 107.

369. 1871. **Rohlfs, Gerard,** von Tripolis nach Alexandrien.—Beschreibung der im Auftrage Sr. Majestät des Königs von Preussen in den Jahren 1868-und 1869 Ausgeführten Reise. Bremen: 8vo, 2 vol. Maps, plates and photographs.

370. 1871. **Nachtigal, Dr.**—Anknuft in Kuka und die Uebergabe der Preussischen Geschenke an den Sultan von Bornu. Peterm. Geogr. Mitth. p. 67.

371. —— Neueste Nachrichten von Dr. N. in Kuka (bis Januar 1871). Ethnographie von Wadai. l. c., p. 327.

372. -—— Notizen über Reise von Murzuk nach Kuka, 18 April bis 6 Juli 1870. l. c., p. 450.

373. —— Briefe aus Nord-Central-Afrika. Zeitsch. der Ges. für Erdk. zu Berlin. 6 Bd. Heft. 8, pp. 130–150.

374. —— Brief des Dr. —— aus Bornu. Das Ausl. Nr. 20, p. 475.

375 —— Brief des Herrn Dr. —— an die Redaktion. Zeitsch. der Ges. für Erdk. zu Berlin. 6 Bd. 4 Heft. pp. 331–315.

376. —— Uebersicht über die Geschichte Wadaï's. l. c., 6 Bd. 4 Heft, pp. 315–366.

377. 1871. Drummond-Hay, Cons.-Gen. F. R.—Report on the trade of Tripoli for 1869. Cons. Comm. Rep. pt. i. p. 295.

378. —— do. for 1870. l. c., pt. ii. p. 1065.

379. —— Report on the condition of the Industrial Classes in the Regency of Tripoli. Rep. from II.M. Diplom. and Cons. Officers, pp. 709.

380. 1871. Henderson, Vice-Consul.—Report on the trade of Bengazi for 1870-71. Cons. Comm. Rep. pt. ii. pp. 1068.

381. 1873. Cosson, E.—Descriptio plantarum novarum in Cyrenaico a G. Rohlfs detectarum. Paris : 8vo, pp. 11.
From Bull. de la Soc. botan. de France, Fév. 1872, t. xix. p. 80.

382. 1873. Halévy, Jos.—Les inscriptions libyques. Article in 'l'Athénée Oriental.' Paris, 1873.

383. 1873. Beulé, M.—Fouilles et découvertes, résumées et discutées en vue de l'histoire de l'art. Paris : 2 vol. 8vo, pp. 430-456.
Vol. ii. p. 59 —Les Ruines de Cyrène. Chap. i. p. 64—Histoire de Cyrène —Ses Ruines. Chap. ii. p. 73—Les Temples de Bacchus et d'Apollon. Chap. iii. p. 80—Temples voisins du Stade ; p. 90—Le Vase de Bérénice.

384. 1873. Drummond-Hay, Con.-Gen. F. R.—Report on the trade of Tripoli for 1871. Cons. Comm. Rep. pt. ii. p. 1328.

385. —— Report on Tripoli. l. c., pt. iii. p. 657.

386. —— Report on the trade of Tripoli for 1872. l. c. p. 1077.

387. 1873. Henderson, Vice-Consul.—Report on the trade of Bengazi for 1872. l. c. p. 1031.

388. 1873. Protocol signed by the Plenipotentiaries of Great Britain and Turkey, respecting Consular Jurisdiction in Tripoli. Hertslet's Treaties, vol. xiv. p. 540.

389. 1873. Dournaux-Dupéré, Norbert.—La rôle de la France dans l'Afrique Septentrionale et la Voyage à Timbouktou. Bull. Soc. Géogr. Paris, 6me sér. t. vi. p. 607.
The author gives a sketch of all that has been done for the exploration of the south, both in Algeria, Tripoli and Morocco ; written as a preliminary study for his projected journey in the Sahara of Algeria, where he was killed in the following year.

390. 1874. Drummond-Hay, Cons.-Gen. Frank.—Report on the trade of Tripoli for 1872. Cons. Comm. Rep. part ii. p. 1077.

391. 1874 Henderson, Vice-Consul.—Report on the trade of Bengazi for 1872. l. c., p. 1080.

392. 1874. Louis-Salvador, Archduke.—Yacht-Reise in den Syrten. 1873. Prag : 4to, pp. 400, with map, 30 illustrations, and 34 woodcuts in text.
This, like all the distinguished author's numerous works, is got up magnificently, and is for private circulation only. His route lay from Alexandria along the North Coast of Africa to Tunis.

393. 1874. Sevestre, H.—D'Alger à Tripoli ; mission de l'aviso le "Kléber," mai et juin 1874. Rev. Mar. et Colon, Dec., pp. 685-782.
The *Kléber* had to visit the coral fisheries and to " show the flag " in Tunis and Tripoli.

394. 1874. **Duveyrier, Henri.**—L'Afrique Nécrologique. Bull. Soc. Géogr. Paris, 6me sér. t. viii. p. 560.

This gives a short account of all who have fallen victims to their endeavours to advance geographical knowledge in Africa, including, of course, the Barbary States. A very instructive map is added, showing the region in which each person travelled and the place of his death.

395. 1874. **Posthumus, N. W.**—Freule Tinne, de Nederlandsche reizigster door Afrika. With 2 maps. Tijdschrift van het Aardrijkskundig Genootschap gevestigd te Amsterdam, No. 3, pp. 72–89.

Biography and travels of Madlle. A. Tinne.

396. 1874–75. **Rohlfs, Gérard.**—Zustände in Berberien, 2e Jahresbericht der Geographischen Gesellschaften. Hamburg.

397. 1875. **Drummond-Hay, Consul-Gen. Frank.**—Report on the trade of Tripoli for 1873. Cons. Comm. Rep., pt. i. p. 599.

398. 1875. **Henderson, Vice-Consul.**—Report on the trade of Bengazi for 1873. l. c., pt. ii. p. 907.

399. 1875. **Gay, Jean.**—Bibliographie des ouvrages relatifs à l'Afrique et à l'Arabie. Catalogue méthodique de tous les ouvrages français et des principaux en langues étrangères, traitant de la géographie, de l'histoire, du commerce, des lettres et des arts de l'Afrique et de l'Arabie. San Remo: 8vo, pp. 312.

This contains only a short list of books on Tripoli and the Cyrenaica.

400. 1875. **Fournel, Henri.**—Les Berbères. Étude sur la conquête de l'Algérie par les Arabes, d'après des textes arabes imprimées. Paris: 4to, t. i. pp. xii. and 609. The second vol. published in 1881, pp. iv. and 381.

The result of long and patient investigation.

401. 1875. **Largeau, V.**—Voyage à Ghadames. Bull. Soc. Géogr. Paris, p. 505, and Globe, t. xiv. pp. 95–119.

The author proceeded viâ Touggourt.

402. —— Voyage dans le Sahara Central. Bull. Soc. Géogr. de Lyon, Jan. pp. 65–89.

403. —— Le commerce du Sahara. L'Explorateur Géogr. et Comm., No. 19, p. 436 et seq.

404. —— Spedizione nel Sahara Centrale. Cosmos, No. vi. p. 201 et seq.

405. 1875. **Rohlfs, Gerhard.**—Paul Soleillet's und Largeau's Reisen in die Sahara und nach dem Sudan. Peterm. Geogr. Mitth. p. 401.

406. 1875. **Mercier, Ernest.** — Histoire de l'Établissement des Arabes dans l'Afrique Septentrionale selon les documents fournis par les auteurs Arabes, et notamment par l'Histoire des Berbères d'ibn Khaldoun. Constantine: 8vo, pp. 406, with map.

407. 1875. **Perk, M. A.**—Zes jaren te Tripoli in Barbarije. Uit de gedenk- schriften eener Nederlandsche Vrouw, door M. A. Perk. Amsterdam: 8vo.

The lady in question was wife of Clifford Koek van Brengel, Dutch Consul at Tripoli from 1827–33, who made an interesting archæological journey in the Cyrenaica.

408. 1876. **Drummond-Hay, Cons.-Gen. Frank.**—Report on the trade of Tripoli for 1874. Cons. Comm. Rep. pt. i. p. 843.

409. 1876. **Henderson, Vice-Cons.**—Report on the trade of Bengazi for 1874. l. c., p. 361.

410. 1876. **Italian Consular Report,** Tripoli. Cenni intorno al commercio, &c. Boll. Consol. pubblicate per cura del Ministero per gli Aff. Est. Torine, vol. xii. p. 219.

411. 1876. **Veth, Prof. P. J.,** and **Dr. C. M. Kars.**—Bibliografic van Nederlandsche Boeken, Brochures, Karten, enz. over Afrika. Utrecht : 8vo, pp. 98. Pp. 18 to 29 are devoted to North Africa.

412. 1876. **Bainier, P.**—La Régence de Tripoli. Avec une Carte. L'Explorateur, No. 58, vol. iii. p. 202.

This is an extract from a work not then published, "Cours de Géographie Commerciale," by the author, who was "Sous-directeur de l'Ecole supérieure de Commerce de Marseille."

413. 1876. **Tripoli.** Article in Larousse, Grand. Dict. Univ. au xix Siècle, t. xv. p. 514.

414. 1876. **Daveaux, J.**—Excursion à Malte et en Cyrénaïque. Paris : 8vo, pp. 8, from the Bull. de la Soc. bot. de France, t. xxiii. 14 Janv.

415. 1876. **Bary, Dr. Edwin von.**—Die Senan oder Megalitischen Denkmäler in Tripolis. Zeitsch. für Ethnologie, Leipzig, Bd. viii. 378-385.

Translated into French by Dr. F. Dargaud, under the title, " Les Senam et les Tumuli de la chaine maritime de la Tripolitaine." Rev. d'Ethnographie, Paris, 1883, t. ii. p. 426-437, fig. 155.

416. —— Voyage dans le Djebel Tripolitain. Explorateur, No. 75.

417. 1876. **Rohlfs, Gerhard.**—Largeau's zweite Expedition nach Rhadames und einige Worte über Algerien. Peterm. Geogr. Mitth. p. 250.

418. 1877. **Tauxier, L.**—Notice sur Corippus et sur la Johannide. Rev. Afr. vol. xx. p. 289.

The Johannide, a Latin poem by Flavius Cresconius, was written in the sixth century, and narrates the exploits of Johannes Troglita, an officer of Justinian, and one of the successors of Belisarius and Salomon in Africa.

419. 1877. **Bary, Dr. E. v.**—Reise in Nord-Afrika. Globus, Bd. xxxii. p. 5 *et seq.*

420. —— Reisebriefe aus Nord-Africa. Zeitschr. Geo. f. Erdk. Berlin. Nos. 3 and 4, pp. 161-199.

421. 1877. **Mouchez, Admiral E.,** Director of the Observatory at Paris.—Explanation des Golfes des deux Syrtes entre Sfax et Benghasi. Comptes-rendues des séances de l'Acad. des Sc. t. lxxxiv. pp. 49-55.

422. —— Exploration de la Grande Syrte. l. c., pp. 97-101.

423. 1877. **Barth, E. v.**—Largeau's erste Reise in Nord-Afrika. Das Ausland. No. 21, pp. 401-409.

424. 1877. **Drummond-Hay, Cons.-Gen. Frank.**—Report on the trade of Tripoli for 1875. Cons. Comm. Rep. pt. ii. p. 940.

425. 1877. **Henderson, Vice-Cons.**—Report on the trade of Bengazi for 1875. l. c., p. 1641.

426. 1877. **Firman** abolishing Slave Trade in Tripoli. Hertslet's Treaties, vol. xv. p. 831.

427. 1877. **The Mediterranean Pilot.**—Compiled from various sources. Published by order of the Lords Commissioners of the Admiralty. London : 8vo.

Vol. ii. pp. 215-255 contains a description of the N. Coast of Africa from Jerbah (Djerba) Island to El-Arish.

428. 1877. Rae, Edward, F.R.G.S.—The Country of the Moors. A Journey from Tripoli in Barbary to the City of Kairwan. London : 8vo, pp. 334, with map and 8 illustrations.

The author visited Tripoli and Lebda, going and returning by sea.

429. 1877. Cyrenaica—Cyrene. Articles in the Encyclopædia Britannica, 9th edition, vol. vi. p. 750.

430. 1877. Bonola, Fredrico.—I Viaggiatori Italiani nell'Africa. V. Viaggiatori Italiani in Berberia, nel Sahara; nel Bornù. Cosmos di Guido Cora, t. iv. p. 21.

431. 1877. Beulé, M., Vase de Bengazi communiqué et expliqué par, — Mém. de l'Instit. Acad. des Inscr. et Bell. Lett. t. xxv. p. 41.

432. 1877. Brunet de Presle, M.—Observations sur le vase de Bengazi. l. c. p. 43.

433. 1877. Beulé, M., Réponse de. l. c. p. 44.

434. 1877. Nachtigal, Dr. G.—Voyage au Wadai (Conférence faite à la Soc. de Géog. de Vienne). Bull. Trim. de la Soc. Khédiviale de Géogr. du Caire, No. 4, Dec. 1876–Avril 1877, pp. 305-350.

435. 1877. Rohlfs, Gerhard.—Eine Eisenbahn nach Central-Africa. Petermann, Geogr. Mitth., p. 45 et seq., with map of the country S. of the Syrtis as far as Murzouk.

436. ——— Die Bedeutung Tripolitaniens an sich und als Ausgangepunkt für Entdeckungsreisende. Weimar : 8vo, map.

437. ——— Die Bedeutung Tripolitaniens an sich und als Ausgangspunkt für Entdeckungsreisende. Weimar : 8vo, pp. 21, with map.

The author maintains that Tripoli is the best place of departure for the Soudan.

438. 1877. Playfair, Sir R. Lambert, K.C.M.G.—Travels in the Footsteps of Bruce in Algeria and Tunis. London : 4to, pp. 300.

Pp. 275 to 294 contain an account of Bruce's Travels in Tripoli and the Cyrenaica, with facsimiles of his drawings of the quadrifrontal arch at Tripoli, and on the outer cover of the volume his drawing of the Doric Columns at Ptolemeta.

439. 1877. Largeau, V.—Voyage dans le Sahara et à Rhadames. Bull. Soc. Géogr. Paris, pp. 35-37. Le Globe, t. xvi. p. 205 ; L'Exploration, No. 41, p. 25 et seq.; Rev. Lyonnaise de Géogr., No. 1, p. 3.

440. 1877. Féraud, L. Charles.—Notes sur un voyage en Tunisie et en Tripolitaine. Rev. Afr. vol. xx. p. 490.

The last few lines only are devoted to Tripoli and Benghazi.

441. 1878. Bossière, Gustave, Inspecteur d'Académie.—Esquisse d'une Histoire de la Conquête et de l'Administration Romaines dans le Nord d'Afrique, et particulièrement dans la Province de Numidie. Paris : 8vo, pp. 436.

There is nothing very especial in this regarding the region east of Tunis, except incidentally as forming part of the Roman possessions.

442. 1878. Rohlfs, Gerhard.—Neues Afrikanisches Forschungs-Unternehmen. With map of country south of Tripoli and the Cyrenaica. Petermann, Geogr. Mitth. p. 20.

443. 1878. Nachtigal, Dr. G.—Von Tripolis nach Fezzân. With original map. Petermann, Geogr. Mitth. p. 45.

444. 1878. **Krause, G. A.**—Cronik von Fesan. Zeitsch. der Gesellschaft für Erdkunde z. Berlin, p. 356.
'A more repetition of Rohlfs, Petermann, Mitth. 1868, p. 1.

445. 1878. **Ayuso, D. F. G.**—Viaje de Rohlfs de Tripoli à Lagos. Madrid: 8vo, pp. 167. From ' Los descubrimientos Geográf. Modernos.'

446. ———— Voyage de Rohlfs de Tripoli à Lagos. Paris : 8vo. pp. 61.

447. 1878. **Drummond-Hay, Cons.-Gen. Frank.**—Report on the trade of Tripoli for 1876. Cons. Comm. Rep. pt. ii. p. 932.

448. 1878. **Henderson, Vice-Cons.**—Report on the trade of Bengazi for 1876. l. c., p. 930.

449. 1879. **Drummond-Hay, Cons.-Gen. Frank.**—Report on the trade of Tripoli for 1877. Cons. Comm. Rep. pt. ii. p. 788.
This gives an account of the esparto trade.

450. 1879. **Rohlfs, Gerhard.**—Notices of his expedition. Petermann, Geogr. Mitth. p. 72 et seq. Cosmos di Guido Cora, vol. v. p. 114 et seq.

451. ———— Reise nach Kufra. Mitth. d. Afrik. Ges. No. 4, p. 12 et seq.

452. ———— Zur Charakteristik der Sahara. Zeitschr. f. Erdk. No. 5, p. 368

453. ———— Die Oase Djofra im Jahre 1879. Westermann's Monatsb. iii. n. 13, p. 80. Also L'Explor, p. 376.

454. ———— Cyrenaïka oder Barka. Geogr. Rundschau, i. n. 12, p. 614.

455. 1879. **Nachtigal, Dr. Gustav.**—Sahara und Sudan. Ergebnisse sechsjähriger Reisen in Afrika. Berlin : 2 vol. 8vo, pp. 748, 790. With numerous illustrations and maps. A most valuable work. The author started from Tripoli, travelling south to Lake Tschad.
Also a French translation by Jules Gourdault. Paris : 8vo, pp. 540, with map and 99 illustrations.
And an Italian one in the Cosmos di Guido Cora, vol. v. p. 411 et seq.
The first nine chapters are devoted to Tripoli and Fezzan.

456. 1879. **Golf von Sidra,** Beschreibung von Untiefer im — Tripolis. Ann. d'Hydrogr. No. 4, p. 181.

457. 1879. **Chavanne, Dr. Josef.**—Die Sahara, oder von Oase zu Oase. Wien : 8vo, pp. 639. With map and many illustrations.
I. Von Tripoli nach Murzuk.
II. Fessan.
III. Von Murzuk nach Rhat.
IV. Von Rhat nach Rhadames, &c.

458. 1879. **Gorringe, Lt.-Commander Henry H.,** and **Lieut. Seaton Schroeder, U.S. Navy.**—Coasts and Islands of the Mediterranean Sea. Bureau of Navigation, Hydrographic Office, Washington : 8vo.
Part iii. pp. 219 to 281 contains a description of the Tripolitan coast as far as the frontiers of Egypt. Two plates, containing sketches of coasts and headlands.

459. 1879. **Paladini, Leone.**—La ferrovia del Sahara, fra Cabes e il Sudan, e sua evidente correlazione cogli interessi commerciali d' Italia. Cagliari : 8vo, pp. 64.

460. 1880. **Drummond-Hay, Cons.-Gen. Frank.**—Report on the trade of Tripoli for 1878. Cons. Comm. Rep. pt. i. p. 600.

461. 1880. **Dupuis, Consul.**—Report on the trade of Bengazi for 1878. l. c., p. 595.

462. 1880. **Jones, Consul.**—Report on the trade of Tripoli, for the quarter ending 30th June, 1880. Reports from the Consuls of the United States, No. 2, p. 2.

463. 1880. **Italian Consular Report** on Tripoli for 1880. Poll. Consolare, pubblicato per cura del Ministero per gli affari Esteri, Roma, vol. xvii. p. 789.

464. 1880. **Puchstein, O.**—Zur Arkesilasschule. Archäol. Zeit. Berlin, 1880, p. 185. On the subject of Cyrenian pottery.

465. 1880. **Bary, E. v.**—Tagebuch, geführt auf seiner Reise von Tripolis nach Ghat und Aïr. Zeitschr. Ges. f. Erdk. Berlin, No. 1.

466. 1880. **Camperio.**—Gita nella Tripolitania. Esplor. vol. ix.—See also Un Viaggio a Tripoli.

467. 1880. **Rohlfs, Gerhard.**—Importanza della Tripolitania per sè stessa e come punto di partenza per gli esploratori. Versione del cap. dott. C. dall'Acqua. L'Esploratore, Giornali di Viaggi e Geografia Commerciale, Milano, anno iv. pp. 387–394.

468. 1880. **Rossoni,** Agente Consolare d'Italia.—La Pesca delle spugne sulle coste di Barberia. Bengasi. l. c. p. 395.
Followed by tables of trade and navigation of Tripoli for 1879.

469. —— Handel und Colonien in Nord-Afrika. Export, No. 22.

470. —— Neue Beiträge zur Entdeckungund Erforschung Afrika. Cassel: 8vo, pp. 159. This specially refers to N. Africa.

471. 1880. **Pasqua, Dr.,** Médecin en Chef de l'Hôpital Militaire de Benghazi. Le Docteur Gerhard Rohlfs et l'expédition allemande en Afrique (1879). Rev. de Géogr. Paris, t. vii. p. 215.
Dr. Rohlfs conveyed presents from the Emperor of Germany to the Sultan of Wadaï in return for the hospitality of the latter to Dr. Nachtigal. He was accompagnied by a naturalist, Dr. A. Stecker.

472. 1881. **Rohlfs, Gerhard.**—Kufra. Reise von Tripolis nach der Oase Kufra, ausgeführt im Auftrage der Afrikanischen Gesellschaft in Deutschland von G. R. Nebst, Beiträgen von P. Ascherson, J. Hann, F. Karsch, W. Peters, A. Stecker. Mit 11 Abbildungen und 3 Karten. Leipzig : 8vo. pp. viii. 559.
Also an Italian translation : Tripolitania, viaggio da Tripoli all' oasi Kufra, by Dr. Guido Cora. Milano : 8vo, pp. 200.
A second part of the work is devoted to scientific subjects, in which he is aided by several distinguished naturalists.
Reviewed in the Rev. des Deux Mondes, by **G. Valbert,** 1st Nov. 1881, under the title " Un voyage malheureux dans les Oasis de la Tripolitaine."

473. —— Neue Beiträge zur Entdeckung und Erforschung Africa's. Cassel : 8vo, pp. 156.
Notes on various subjects ; inter alia on Halfa grass, and the importance of Tripoli in the problem of opening out Africa.

474. 1881. **Ascherson, P.**—Florula der Oasengruppe Kufra nach den Beobachtungen und Sammlungen von G. Rohlfs. Sitzungsber d. Botan. Vereins d. Prov. Brandenburg, xxiii.—See also Rohlf's Kufra (1881).

475. 1881. **Kraus, Dr.**—Dell' Oasi et Città di Ghat. L'Esploratore, An. v. p. 73 et seq. with plan.

476. 1881. **Bottiglia, Cap. G.**—Rapporto da Bengasi. l. c., p. 104.
Followed by statistics of commerce in Tripoli during 1880.

477. 1881. **Camperio, Cap. M.**—Una Gita in Cirenaica. l. c., p. 257 *et seq.*
with map.

478. 1881. **Mamoli, P.**—Atti e Notizie Bengazi-Derna. l. c., pp. 277-406.

479. 1881. **Puchstein, O.**—Kyrenaeische Vasen. Archäol. Zeit. Berlin, 1881,
p. 317, pl. 10-13.
An article intended to prove that a certain class of vases, of which the
Arkesilaos vase of Paris is a well-known example, were manufactured in the
6th century. For engraving of that vase see title-page Birch's Ancient
Pottery, 1873.

480. 1881. **Gorringe, H. H.**—A Cruise along the Northern Coast of Africa.
Bull. Amer. Geogr. Soc. No. 2, pp. 47-58.

481. 1881. **Bisson, Léon de.**—La Tripolitaine et la Tunisie, avec les renseignements indispensables au voyageur. Paris: 8vo, pp. 147.
A very superficial work.

482. 1881. **Perrond, Cl.**—De Syrticis emporiis, thesim facultate litterarum
parisiensi proponebat ad doctoris gradum promovendus Cl. P——. Parisiis: 8vo.,
pp. 226.
To this is joined, Index operum in hac commendatione laudatorum—about
109 entries.

483. 1881. **Cherbonneau, A.**—Ghadames et le Commerce Soudanien. Rev. de
Géogr. Juin.

484. 1881.' **Richard, P. L., Missionnaire.**—Carte du Sahara Tripolitain pour
servir à l'intelligence d'un voyage chez les Touaregs Azghers. Les Missions
Catholiques. Lyon: t. 13. No text.

485. 1881. **Consular Report (Italian)** on Tripoli. Boll. Consol. xviii. p. 3.

486. 1881. **Skippen, E., Medical Director, U.S. Navy.**—A forgotten General.
The United Service; a monthly review of military and naval affairs, Philadelphia,
vol. v. No. 1, p. 1.
Gives an account of the filibustering expedition of William Eaton, the well-
known American "General" in the Cyrenaica. He was named U.S. Consul at
Tunis. After a short and troubled residence there he proceeded to Egypt,
whence he marched with an ill-assorted and mutinous force to Derna, which
he took, though he was speedily obliged to evacuate it.

487. 1881. **Wilmanns, Gustavus.**—Inscriptiones Africae Latinae consilio et
auctoritate Academiae Litterarum Regiae Borussiae. Collegit G. W. Berolini:
2 vol. folio.
Part 1, pp. 1-9 contains inscriptions collected in the Province of Tripoli.

488. 1881. **Brunialti, Dr. Attilio.**—Algeria, Tunisia e Tripolitania, studio di
geografia politica sugli ultimi avvenimenti africani. Milano: 12mo, pp. 274,
map.
Reviewed in the Bull. Corres. Afr. 1884, p. 147.
The author seeks to turn the eyes of his countrymen to this country, which
he believes destined to become a new Italy.

489. 1881. **Bottiglia, Capt.**—Lettera da Bengasi. L'Esploratore, No. 8,
pp. 277-280.

490. 1881. **Haimann, Comm.**, and **S. Pastore.**—Da Bengasi a Derna. L' Esploratore, No. 7, pp. 251–253.

Haimann's work was published separately at Milan in 1886. q. v.

491. 1881. **Mamoli, P.**—La Cirenaica. L' Esploratore, No. 7, pp. 241–251.

492. ——— Lettere da Derna. l. c., No. 8, pp. 280–288.

493. 1881. **Reisen in Cyrenaica.**—Im Auftrage der Handels-Erforschungs-gesellschaft von Mailand ausgeführt von Capitän Camperio und Dr. Mamoli, Commendatore Haimann und Herrn Pastore. Petermann, Geogr. Mitth. pp. 321, with map of the Cyrenaica.

494. 1881. **Drummond-Hay, Cons.-Gen. F. R.**—Report on the trade of Tripoli for 1880. Cons. Comm. Rep. pt. i. p. 373.

495. ——— Report on the trade of Tripoli for 1879. l. c., pt. i. p. 993.

496. 1881. **Dupuis, Consul.**—Report on the trade of Bengazi for 1879. l. c., p. 1601.

497. 1882. **Playfair, Sir R. Lambert, K.C.M.G.**—Handbook (Murray's) to the Mediterranean, its cities, coasts and islands. London: 8vo.

Pp. 43 to 49 contain an account of the Coast of Tripoli and the Cyrenaica.

498. 1882. **Broadley, A. M.**—The last Punic War—Tunis past and present, with a narrative of the French Conquest of the Regency. London: 2 vol. 8vo. pp. 356, 398, with illustrations.

Chap. xl. vol. ii. p. 219 contains a description of "Tripoly in the West" and of the Confraternity of Es-Senoussi.

499. 1882. **Drude, Dr. Oscar.**—Die floristische Erforschung Nord-Afrika's von Marokko bis Barka. Petermann, Geogr. Mitth. pp. 143–150.

At the end of this article is a short notice of the flora of Tripoli and Barca.

500. 1882. **Ascherson, P.**, Professor at Berlin.—Note Botaniche intorno ad alcune piante dell' Africa Boreale alta alla concia delle pelli. L' Esploratore, an. vi. p. 358.

501. 1882. **Camperio, Capit.**—Notizie Statistiche su Barca (Cirenaica). Da una Relazione del Capitano Camperio pubblicata dalla Mittheilungen di Gotha (1881). l. c., p. 366.

502. 1882. **Mamoli, P.**—Stazione di Derna, della Soc. d' Esplor. Comm. in Africa, Rapporto No. 35 del delegato P. Mamoli. l. c., p. 367.

503. 1882. **N. N.**—A Proposito della Tripolitania. l. c., p. 397.

504. 1882. **Fontpertuis, Ad. F. de.**—Géographie. La Tripolitaine, le Fezzan et le Tibesté. Rev. Scient. Paris, 3me sér. t. iii. p. 775.

505. 1882. **Mamoli.**—Stazioni di Derna (Cirenaica). Cenni storici e geografici L'Esploratore, an. vi. p. 68.

506. 1882. **Bottiglia, G.**—Relazione sull' importazione ed esportazione di Bengase, anno 1881. l. c., p. 70.

507. 1882. **Bettoli, Parmenio.**—Tripoli Artistica. l. c., Fasc. iii. et seq.

In the same number is a map of the territory of Bengazi.

508. ——— Tripoli Commerciale. l. c., pp. 265 et seq.

509. 1882. **Mamoli, P.**—Stazione di Derna. Gita alle fonti. l.c., pp. 196 and 324.

510. —— L' incidente di Derna l. c., p. 218. The arrest of Sig. Mamoli, agent of the Società d'Esplorazione at Ras-et-Tin, near Derna.

511. 1882. **Haimann, G.**—Cirenaica, con disegni dell' autore. Boll. Soc. Geogr. Ital. vii. No. 1, p. 6.—See also L' Esploratore, An. vi. p. 306.

Haimann and Camperio made a journey in the Cyrenaica, accompanied by the wife of the former and a numerous escort.

512. 1882. **Schweiger-Lerchenfeld, A. von.**—Der Orient. Wien: 8vo, pp. cxlii. 808.

Copiously illustrated. P. 793 to the end devoted to Tripoli and Tunis.

513. 1882. **Tripoli—Prezzi correnti** delle merci. Boll. Consol. vol. xviii. p. 586.

514. —— Another short notice. l. c., p. 322.

515. —— Movimento della navigazione. l. c., vol. xix. p. 252.

516. 1882. **Rohlfs, G.**—Die Kufra-Oase. Westermann's Monatshefte, l. l., N. 306, pp. 785-795.

517. —— Liegt ein Grund vor, die Städtebevölkerung von Marokko, Algerien, Tunisien und Tripolitanien als eine besondere zu betrachten und zu benennen? Ausland: N. 16, pp. 301-307.

518. 1882. **Bettoli, P.**—Tripoli commerciale. L' Esploratore, vi. No. 7, pp. 265-273. With map.

518A. 1882. **Paulitschke, Dr. Philippe.**—Die Afrika-Literatur in der Zeit von 1500 bis 1750, N. Ch. Ein Beitrag zur geographischen Quellenkunde. Gelegentlich des ii. Deutschen Geographentages zu Halle a/S.

Wien : 8vo. pp. 122.

Of the 1212 works here catalogued, 450 have reference to Egypt and North Africa.

518B. 1882. **Splaine, J. F.**—Four days in Tripoli. "The Month" : vol. xliv. p. 91, January, 1882. See also Liv. Age. vol. clii. p. 312.

519. 1883. **Charmes, Gabriel.**—La Tunisie et la Tripolitaine. Paris: 8vo, pp. 443, 2nd Ed. in 1884.

This work is a reproduction of letters which appeared in the Journal des Débats in July and Aug. 1882. The author visited Tripoli during the Insurrection in Egypt, when great agitation existed in the West.

520. 1883. **Duveyrier, Henri.**—Tremblement de terre à Ghalames. Compte Rend. Soc. Géogr. Paris, p. 454.

521. 1883. **Feraud, L. Charles.**—Annales Tripolitaines. Lettre de M. F., Consul-Général de France à Tripoli, à M. de Grammont, Président de la Soc. hist. Alg. Rev. Afr. vol. xxvii. p. 207.

The author gives a short account of Tripoli from 1146, when Roger, King of Sicily, took possession of it, and he appends a list of the various French consuls from 1630. He promises a more complete work afterwards. M. Feraud died at Tangier while these sheets were in the press.

522. 1883. **Rizetto, R.**—Attached to the Ministry of Foreign Affairs. La Tripolitania quale risulta dai viaggi di G. Rohlfs. Roma: pp. 128.

Reviewed by F. C. in the 'Nuova Antologia' of 15th Jan. This work cites the opinion of Rohlfs, that Italy should conquer the Cyrenaica.

523. 1883. **Rizetto, R.**—I commerci di Tripoli e quelli del Sudan. Roma: 8vo, pp. 118.
Estratto dai Giornale Il Diritto.

524. 1883. **Rohlfs, Gerhard.**—Die Anzahl der Juden in Afrika. Petermann, Geogr. Mitth. p. 211.
Brunialti's estimate of 100,000 Jews in Tripoli is quoted and disproved.

525. 1883. **Lemay, G.**—La Tripolitaine et le Grand Désert. Bull. de la Soc. de Géogr. Comm. t. v. pp. 352–369.
The substance of an address given before the society, based on a residence of several months in the country. The author particularly describes Tripoli and its commerce.

526. 1883. **Cyclop.**—Aus den Beiseberichten S. M. S————, Kapt. Lieut. **Kelch.** Bemerkungen über die Bucht von Tobruk, Nordküste von Afrika. Annalen d. Hydrogr. xi. N. 7, pp. 403–405.

527. 1883. **Schweinfurth, Dr. G.**—La Côte de la Marmarique. Lettre à M. Henri Duveyrier. Compte Rend. Soc. Géog. Paris, p. 484.
The author made a voyage on board a German gunboat to the port of Tobruk. He remarks that he is proud of being the first to call the attention of the Italians to the Cyrenaica and the Tripolitaine.

528. ———— Una Visita al Porto di Tobruc (Cirenaica). L' Esplor. vii. p. 207.
With a plan.

529. 1883. **Mamoli, P.**—Stazione di Derna (Cirenaica). Rapporto 39 del delegato P. M. L' Esploratore, an. vii. p. 29.

530. ———— Rapporto 40. l. c., p. 100.

531. ———— Relazione Agricolo-Commerciale. Report on the operations of the Soc. d' Esplor. Comm. in Africa, especially regarding commerce and colonisation in the Cyrenaica. l. c. vii. p. 193.

532. ———— Rapporto 41. Tobruk. l. c., p. 163.

533. 1883. **Freund, Dr. G. A.**—Viaggio lungo la gran Sirte da Bengasi a Tripoli, Maggio e Giugno, 1881. l. c., pp. 183 et seq.

534. 1883. **Corbetta, Dr. C.**—Da Tripoli ad Algeri. l. c., p. 265.

535. 1883. **Drummond-Hay, Cons.-Gen. Frank.**—Report on the trade of Tripoli for 1881. Cons. Comm. Rep. pt. i. p. 241.

536. 1883. **Italian Consular Report.**—Tripoli. Quadro della Navigazione. Boll. Consol. vol. xx. p. 321.

537. 1884. **Waille, Victor.**—Bibliographie des ouvrages concernant la Cyrénaïque et la Tripolitaine. Alger Bull. Corresp. Afr. p. 227.
The author quotes 127 works on these countries.

538. ———— Recents Travaux Italiens sur la Cyrénaïque. l. c., p. 116.

539. 1881. **Lanier, L.**—L'Afrique. Choix de lectures de Géographie, accompagnées de résumés, d'analyses, de notes explicatives et bibliographiques, et ornées de 57 vignettes, de 9 cartes tirées en couleur et de 33 cartes dans le texte. Paris : 12mo, pp. 920.
Livre ii. p. 345, Région Tripolitaine et Saharienne. At p. 362 is a short bibliography.

540. 1884. **Tissot, Charles,** Ambassador.—Exploration Scientifique de la Tunisie. Géographie Comparée de la Province Romaine d'Afrique. Paris : vol. i. 4to, pp. 697.

At p. 210 is a hydrographical description of the coast of Tripoli.

541. 1884. **Duveyrier, H.**—La Confrérie musulmane de Sidi Mohammed ben 'Ali Es-Senousi et son domaine géographique en l'année 1300 de l'Hegire (1883 de notre ère). Paris : 8vo, pp. 84, with map. From Bull. Soc. de Géogr. Paris, 7ᵉ sér. t. v. pp. 145-226.

542. 1884. **Buonfanti.**—Reise von Tripolis nach Lagos. Peterm. Geogr. Mitth. pp. 272, 314.

543. ———— Le Sahara et le Soudan occidental. Bull. Soc. R. Géogr. Bruxelles, viii. Nos. 1 and 2, with map.

544. 1884. **Camperio, Capt.**—Carta economica della Tripolitania e Cirenaica. This map has been published by the Soc. d' Esplorazione Comm. in Africa, Milano—scale, 1 : 3500,000—and includes all the recent observations of Captain Camperio and his companion, Sr. Mamoli.—See L' Esploratore, an. viii. p. 64.

545. 1884. **Longo, il Pastore P.**—Lo Snussiomo, ovvero la confraternità Mussulmana di Sidi Mohammed Ben Ali es-Snussi. 1. c., p. 121 et seq.

546. 1884. **Brunialti, Prof. A.**—Assab e Tripoli. 1. c., p. 257.

547. 1884. **Garcin, I.**—Tripoli. Corrispondenza commerciale. 1. c., p. 326.

548. 1884. **Schweiger-Lerchenfeld, A. von.**—La Tripolitaine et l'Egypte d'après l'ouvrage allemand de.....par F. Kohn-Abrest. Paris : 8vo, pp. 187, with illustrations.

549. 1884. **Drummond-Hay, Cons.-Gen. Frank.**—Report on the trade of Tripoli for 1882. Cons. Comm. Rep. pt. i. p. 211.

550. 1885. **Melon, Paul.**—De Palerme à Tunis, par Malte, Tripoli et la Côte. Paris : 8vo, pp. 212, 8 illustrations.

This is a mere record of a tourist's impressions. The author states in his preface :—" Ceci n'est pas un livre à proprement parler."

551. 1885. **Piesse, L.**—De la Goulette à Tripoli. Bull. Trim. de Géogr. (Oran) t. v. pp. 8 to 16, 5 illust.

The author simply made the voyage in the mail steamer.

552. 1885. **Longo, Pastore P.**—Delle Antiche Città della Tripolitania. L' Esploratore, an. ix. p. 109.

An attempt to fix the position of the ancient cities after Vivien de St. Martin.

553. 1885. **Camperio, Capt., and Dr. Schweinfurth.**—Sudan, Egitto e Tripolitania. 1. c., p. 169.

554. 1885. **Brunialti, Prof. A.**—Andiamo a Tripoli ? 1. c., p. 210.

Extracted from the author's work, ' L' Italia e la questione coloniale,' Milano, 1885. This gives a succinct account of the Tripolitaine and the Cyrenaica, and the benefits likely to result to Italy from the possession of these countries.

555. 1885. **La Tratta degli Schiavi** in Tripolitania. 1. c., p. 256.

556. 1885. **Lupi.** La Tripolitania. Rome.

A work of no particular scientific merit, but intended to make known the country in Italy, and to advocate its occupation by that nation.

557. 1885. **La Cirenaica (Tripolitania).**

The anonymous author reviews the work of Giuseppe Haimann (2nd ed. w'th plans of Bengazi and Derna), and suggests that the Italian Government should assist the Milanese Society in exploring the country.   Nuova Antologia, 1st November.

557A. 1885. **Elisyeër, A. V.**—Anthropological Expedition into the Sahara through Tripoli, Tunis and Algiers (Russian).

Izvyestiya Imperatorskova Russkova Geographicheskovo obschestva. St. Petersburg. T. xxi. No. 4.

558. 1885. **Drummond-Hay, Cons.-Gen. Frank.**—Report on the trade of Tripoli for 1883. Cons. Comm. Rep. pt. i. p. 360.

559. 1885. **Wood, Consul.**—Report on trade of Bengazi for 1883. l. c., p. 1389.

560. 1886. **Reclus, Élisée.**—Nouvelle Géographie Universelle ; La Terre et les Hommes. T. xi.—L'Afrique Septentrionale : Tripolitaine, Tunisie, Algérie Maroc, Sahara. Paris, 8vo, pp. 912, 4 coloured maps, 160 maps in the text, and 83 woodcuts.

A work of the highest value. The portion devoted to Tripoli and the Cyrenaica is from p. 1 to 133.

561. 1886. **Estournelles de Constant, P. d'.**—Les Sociétés secrètes chez les Arabes et la conquête de l'Afrique du Nord. Rev. des Deux Mondes, March, t. lxxiv. p. 100.

Gives an account of the order of Es-Senoussi in the Cyrenaica.

562. 1886. **Mas-Latrie, le Comte de.**—Relations et Commerce de l'Afrique Septentrionale ou Magreb, avec les Nations Chrétiennes au moyen âge. Paris : 12mo, pp. 550.

Pp. 384-389 especially devoted to Genoese relations with Tripoli in 1355.

563. ——— Anciens Évêchés de l'Afrique Septentrionale. Bull. Corresp. Afr. 5e year, p. 80.

This is a re-arrangement of the sees given by Morcelli, in geographical order. Eight are mentioned as in the Tripolitaine.

564. 1886. **Rohlfs, Gerhard.**—Quid novi ex Africa ? Cassel : 8vo, pp. vii. 288.

A series of detached papers, one of which is, "Is there any reason for believing that the town population of Morocco, Algeria, Tunis and Tripoli are of a special character?"

565. 1886. **Haimann, Comdt. Giuseppe.**—Cirenaica (Tripolitania). Milano : 8vo, pp. 215, copiously illustrated, also map of the Cyrenaica and plans of Bengazi and Derna.

The author died at Alexandria (1883) before the publication of this work.— See also Peterm. Geogr. Mitth. p. 186.

566. 1886. **Esplorazione Commerciale.**—At the end of 1885 the "Esploratore" was replaced by the above-named journal as the official organ of the "Società d'Esplorazione Commerciale in Africa, Residente in Milano." Frequent letters containing commercial and political information regarding Tripoli and the Cyrenaica continue to appear in it.

567. 1886. **Drummond-Hay, Cons.-Gen. Frank.**—Report on the trade of Tripoli for 1884. Cons. Comm. Rep. pt. i. p. 481.

568. 1887. **Gürich, Dr.**—Ueberblick über den geologischen Bau des Afrikanischen Kontinents. Mit Karte, s Tafel 13. Peterm. Geogr. Mitth. p. 257.

569. 1887. **Fournel, Marc.**—La Tripolitaine, les Routes du Soudan. Paris : 8vo, pp. 272.
Contains much useful information regarding the country, its people, climate and productions.

570. 1887. **Head, Barclay V.**, Assistant Keeper of Coins, Brit. Mus.—Historia Numiarum : a manual of numismatics. Oxford : 8vo, pp. 784.
At page 725 is an account of the coins of the Cyrenaïca, Libya and Syrtica.

571. 1887. **Drummond-Hay, Cons.-Gen. Frank.**—Report on the trade of Tripoli for 1886. Cons. Rep. New Series, No. 89.

572. 1888. **Broadley, A. M.**—Tripoli : article in Enc. Brit., vol. xxiii. p. 574.

573. 1888. **Testa, Jhr. F.**—Waarm. Consul-Generaal le Tripoli. Verslag over 1887. Verz ameling van Consulaire, &c. Jaargang, 1888, p. 588.

574. 1888. **Mauprix, Ch. de.**—Les Italiens à Tripoli. Art. in Le Correspondant, Oct. 10, 1888.

575. 1888. **Les Allemands à Tripoli.**—Rev. Franç. de l'Étr. et des Colon. t. vii. p. 585.

576. 1888. **Tripolitaine.**—Situation économique. l. c., t. viii. p. 165.

577. 1888. **Tripoli,** Commerce. l. c., p. 283.

578. 1888. **Borsari Ferdinando.**—Geografia, Etnologica e Storica della Tripolitania, Cirenaica e Fezzan, con Cenni sulla Storia di queste Regioni e sul Silfio della Cirènaica. Torino; Napoli ; Palermo : 8vo, pp. 278.
This is divided into four parts, each preceded by a short bibliography : i. Geografia Etnologica, pp. 9–66; ii. Geografia Storica, pp. 67–214 ; iii. Cenni sulla Storia della Tripolitania e Cirenaica, pp. 215–268 ; iv. Il Silfio della Cirenaica, pp. 269–279.

579. 1889. **Marbeau, Edouard.**—L'Italie dans l'Afrique du Nord. l. c., t. ix. p. 129, with map.
This contains views favourable to the annexation of Tripoli and the Cyrenaica by Italy. " Nous croyons que la cause de la Civilisation et de la liberté ne ferait que gagner si la France et l'Italie poursuivraient . . . &c."

PUBLIC RECORDS.—TRIPOLI ARCHIVES.

In the Public Record Office in London there is a series of 62 MS. volumes containing correspondence from and to the Consulate-General of Tripoli, as follows:—

Royal Letters, 1590–1742. This volume contains letters and translations from the Beys of Tripoli and Tunis to the Sovereigns of England.

No. 1. 1590–1728. Letters from Consuls Samuel Tooker, Nathaniel Bradley, Admiral Sir John Narborough, Consuls Thomas Baker and Nathaniel Lodington. At the beginning of the vol. is a very curious view of Tripoli (about 1560) being attacked by the Army "del Re Philippo et con aiuto della Sede Apostolica, del Duca de Fiorenza et del gran Mastro della Religion di Rhoda." It also contains printed copies of Sir John Narborough's treaty of 5th March 1675–6.

No. 2. 1659 to Geo. II. An unbound collection of miscellaneous letters.

No. 3. 1729–1746. Letters from Consuls Nathaniel Lodington and William Reed.

No. 4. A single Turkish letter sealed Mohammed ben Othman [A.H.] 1169.

No. 5. 1747–1766. Letters from Consuls William Reed and Robert White.

No. 5 [sic]. 1756–1765. Letters from Consul Robert White and several from the Bey to the King.

No. 6. 1765–1769. Letters from Consuls A. Fraser, Robert Wilkie and Edward Barker.

No. 7. 1770–1779. Letters from Consuls Barker, Bayntun, Cooke, Mr. (afterwards Consul) Tully and others. An unbound collection.

No. 8. 1780–1792. Letters from Consuls Richard Tully and George Burgall.

No. 9. 1793–1804. Letters from Consuls Richard Tully and Simon Lucas, Pro-Consul B. McDonogh and Consul William Wass Langford.

No. 10. 1805–1809. Letters from Consul William Wass Langford.

No. 11. 1810–11. Ditto.

No. 12. 1812–13. Ditto, and from Pro-Cons. Pat. Wilkie and James Somerville.

No. 13. 1814–15. Letters from Cons.-Gen. Colonel Hanmer Warrington.

No. 14. 1816. Ditto.

No. 15. 1817. Ditto.

No. 16. 1818. Ditto.

No. 17. 1819. Ditto. This contains news of Mr. Ritchie's expedition, and letters from him.

No. 18. 1820. Cons.-Gen. Warrington. This contains a coloured sketch of his house, and pencil sketches of antiquities found by him.

No. 19. 1821. Cons.-Gen. Warrington. The first despatch reports transmission of thirty cases of antiquities.

No. 20. 1822. Cons.-Gen. Warrington. Contains a historical memoir on Tripoli, and letters from, and information regarding Dr. Oudney, Capt. Beechey and Mr. A'Court.

No. 21. 1823. Cons.-Gen. Warrington. News of, and letters from Clapperton, Denham and Oudney.

No. 22. 1824. Cons.-Gen. Warrington. Letters from Denham and Toole.

No. 23. 1825. Cons.-Gen. Warrington. Further news of the above travellers, also of Major Laing. An account of Tyrwhitt's death at Bornou.

No. 24. 1825. Cons.-Gen. Warrington. News from Clapperton, Denham and Laing. Antiquities and Greek inscriptions from Cyrene.

No. 25. 1827. Cons.-Gen. Warrington, and Vice-Cons. Dupuis.

No. 26. 1827. Ditto. Letters concerning Major Laing's mission.

No. 27. 1828. Cons.-Gen. Warrington. Consular Diary. News from Clapperton and Denham's mission. Murder of Major Laing.

No. 28. 1828. Cons.-Gen. Warrington. Trade Reports.

No. 29. 1829. Cons.-Gen. Warrington and Vice-Cons. Dupuis. Trade Returns.

No. 30. 1829. Cons.-Gen. Warrington. Letters regarding Major Laing's papers, and Miscellaneous.

No. 31. 1830. Cons.-Gen. Warrington and Vice-Cons. J. Fraser. Consular Diary. French treaty with Tripoli. British convention. Information regarding the murder of Major Laing, and death of Mrs. Laing.

No. 32. 1830. Cons.-Gen. Warrington and Vice-Cons. J. Fraser. Commission to enquire into the charge against French Consul-General for having fraudulently obtained the papers of Major Laing. French expedition under Adm. Rosamel to Tripoli.

No. 32A. 1675-1818. Treaties with Tripoli. Copies made by Cons.-Gen. Warrington.

No. 32B. 1695-1830. Copies of Treaties.

No. 33. 1831. Cons.-Gen. Warrington and Vice-Cons. Fraser. Consular Diary. Letter of Gräberg da Hemsö regarding missing copy of Ibn Batuta.

No. 34. 1831. Cons.-Gen. Warrington. Miscellaneous and Trade returns.

No. 35. 1832. Cons.-Gen. Warrington. Consular Diary of Bengazi. Miscellaneous. Trade returns.

No. 36. 1832. Ditto. Miscellaneous.

No. 37. 1832. Regarding the charge made by the Pasha of Tripoli against Sidi Hassuna D'Ghies of having abstracted the papers of the late Major Laing.

No. 38. 1833. Cons.-Gen. Warrington. Miscellaneous.

[No. 39. Missing.]

No. 40. 1833. Vice-Cons. J. Fraser and Joseph Dupuis. Continuation of the affair of Hassuna D'Ghies and the late Major Laing.

No. 41. 1834. Cons.-Gen. Warrington. Miscellaneous.

No. 42. 1835. Cons.-Gen. Warrington. Miscellaneous.

No. 43. 1835. Cons.-Gen. Warrington. Miscellaneous.

No. 1. 1825-32. Letters to Cons.-Gen. Warrington from Colonial Office.

No. 2. 1832-36. Ditto.

No. 3. 1825-34. Domestic. Answers to letters.

No. 4. 1834-36. Ditto. Ditto.

No. 1. Jan. to Sep., 1836. Letters from Cons.-Gen. Warrington. Diplomatic and Consular.

No. 2. Oct.-Dec., 1836. Ditto. Ditto.

No. 3. 1836. Vice-Cons. Wood, Bengazi and Vice-Cons. Dupuis. Report from the latter on trade of interior, with map.

No. 4. 1837. Cons.-Gen. Warrington and Vice-Cons. Wood, Bengazi.

No. 5. Cons.-Gen. Warrington. Various.

No. 6. Cons.-Gen. Warrington and Vice-Cons. Wood.

No. 7. 1839. Cons.-Gen. Warrington. Various.

No. 8. 1840. Cons.-Gen. Warrington and Vice-Cons. Wood, Bengazi.

No. 9. 1841. Ditto, ditto.

No. 10. 1824-41. Case of Captain Chatten, "La Fortuna."

No. 11. 1842. Cons.-Gen. Warrington.

No. 12. 1842. Ditto. Vice-Cons. Wood, Bengazi.

There are also scattered notices concerning Tripoli, some of great historical interest, in the various printed calendars of State papers published under the direction of the Master of the Rolls, as follows:—

Spanish Series, vol. 1509-1525, pp. 276, 583.

Venetian Series, vol. 1520-1526, No. 796-799.

Foreign and Domestic Series, Henry VIII., vol. i. 1509-1511, No. 1209, and vol. ix. 1535, No. 910.

Foreign Series, Edw. VI., 1547-1553, pp. 157, 162, 163, 165, 168, 170, 172, 175, 183.

Calendar of Treasury Papers, vol. 1556-7-1696, No. 392, 464, 483-542; vol. 1697-1701-2, xlvii. 30, li. 54, lxi. 1, lxv. 9, lxxvii. 36, 57; vol. 1702-1707, lxxxiv. 33, 34, 90, lxxxv. 125, lxxxvi. 19, 100; vol. 1708-1714, cxxxiii. 9, cxxxiv. 61, clx. 24, clxxiii. 24; vol. 1714-19, clxxxiv. 28, clxxxv. 43, clxxxvi. 16, clxxxvii. 44, cxc. 60, cxcii. 41, cxcix. 44, 45, 53, cciv. 63.

Foreign Series, vol. 1559-60, Nos. 550(6), 590(6), 640(3), 665, 859(13), 1066(4); vol. 1560-61, 74(3), 128(3), 148(1, 3, 5), 167(1), 187(1), 194(1, 2), 224(2, 10), 252(6), 328(2), 433(2, 3, 5), 450(3), 564(3), 716(30); vol. 1561-62, 13(2), 256(2), 300; vol. 1564-65, 171(3), 1168(2), 1220(1).

Domestic Series, vol. 1547-1580, p. 551; vol. 1566-1579, p. 563; vol. 1581-1590, pp. 147, 243; vol. 1591-1594, pp. 58, 67, 89; vol. 1595-1597, p. 353; vol. 1601-1603; addenda, 1547-1565, pp. 151, 160; vol. 1603-1610, p. 216; vol. 1633-1634, p. 357; vol. 1651, p. 291; vol. 1651-1652, p. 482; vol. 1652-1653, pp. 44, 58, 118, 119, 120 134, 342; vol. 1653-1654, pp. 42, 130, 137, 167, 213, 250, 263, 288, 289, 487; vol. 1654, pp. 402, 456; vol. 1655, pp. 138, 482; vol. 1655-1656, p. 155; vol. 1656-1657, pp. 8, 272; vol. 1657-1658, pp. 24, 55, 95, 96, 259, 308; vol. 1658-1659, pp. 88-92, 108, 140, 197; vol. 1659-1660, pp. 140, 254, 337, 406, 440; vol. 1660-1661, pp. 43, 586; vol. 1661-1662, pp. 46-58; vol. 1663-1664, p. 385; vol. 1666-1667, p. 483; vol. 1760-1765, Nos. 380, 609, 623, 1518, 1608, 1688, 1837, 1928, 1962, 1993, 1994, 1995, 2009, 2045, 2075; vol. 1766-1769, Nos. 40, 98, 123, 176, 225, 226, 229, 242, 253, 274, 277, 284, 569, 713, 904, 918, 1005, 1100; vol. 1770-1772, Nos. 55, 209, 1002, 1533, p. 626.

INDEX OF SUBJECTS.

N.B.—The figures in this Index refer to the Numbers of the entries in the Bibliography.

INDEX OF AUTHORS.

—•◇•—

N.B.—The figures in this Index refer to the Numbers of the entries in the Bibliography.

C... or Candia

N S E A

Mirsa Susa
APOLLONIA
Ras el Hilal
Derna DARNIS
Ras el Tin
RU Kirrna CYRENE
Nora Gulf of Bomba
Augur Ras el Kenit
Augurbu Mirsa Tobruk Tabarka
AW Reads
CYRENAICA Ras el Milh Mellah
D H A R A B I Gulf of Milh Mirsa Solum
Ajdabia Ras Halam Gasr Shamu
Wadir Laquas 'Rabia

Kambi MARMARICA
Plateau of the Libyan Desert 500 to 600 feet
Limestone Gar ed Dih

Garatrossa
I Hattich Jarabub Abu Tartur
Tariniah Oasis Gur el Laban
Su Furiing Gerdoba TarelGhah Mashu Garah
Timu Teunek Ghashab stluibe Oasis of Garah
Belgela Maragh wells
Battiari Siwah J Hadima
Oasis of Siwah Arai Oasis
Jupiter Ammon Sittrah L
I aush 100
Bahreyn Oasis
300

L A N D E S E R T
Sand with dunes 300 ft high
Oasis of Zerzurah
720

Bu Stghen
Ksebah
ur
a s e s I Sighen
erma Busenna
of Gar Siddel el Abul

MAP OF
AND THE CYRENAICA
accompany the Bibliography of
HE BARBARY STATES
r R. Lambert Playfair, K.C.M.G.

Scale of Statute Miles.
0 100 200

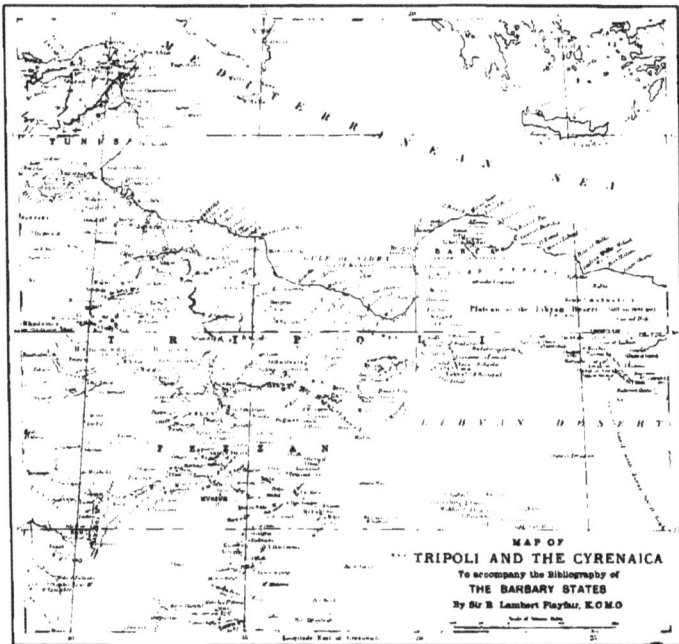

MAP OF
TRIPOLI AND THE CYRENAICA
To accompany the Bibliography of
THE BARBARY STATES
By Sir R. Lambert Playfair, K.C.M.O.

Form L9-17m-8,'55(B303984)444

University of Ca
Southern Reg
Library Faci